From A 𝔐oth
To A 𝔅utterfly

Us As A Family: Sue, Noel, William, Michael, Thomas

From A Moth To A Butterfly

A Journey of Autism

By
Susan Smith Carey

Strategic Book Publishing and Rights Co.

Strategic Book Publishing and Rights Co., LLC
USA | Singapore
www.sbpra.com

For information about special discounts for bulk purchases, please contact Strategic Book Publishing and Rights Co. Special Sales, at bookorder@sbpra.net

ISBN: 978-1-63135-379-6

Book Design by Julius Kiskis

23 22 21 22 20 19 18 17 16   1 2 3 4 5

Acknowledgments

I want to say a huge thankyou to my husband Noel
and my lovely three lads,
Thomas, Michael and William.
All of whom have helped me with this book
in their own personal way.

To my family, my Mam and Dad, my brothers, sisters, in-laws,
partners and close friends, to all of you who have helped me
through some very tough times, including my sister Marie
who passed away, I want to acknowlede and thank you all for
everyones non judgemental continuous love
and support over the years.

I would like to acknowledge SBPRA, with its many
departments and thank them all for publishing my book, you
were all very patient and supportive
throughout this production.

Prologue

This book has been collaborated from notes I have written in my diary to release my frustration. It is about my many-year ordeal with my three precious sons who were diagnosed with autism spectrum disorder (ASD), what we went through as a family, and the hard struggle we waged to get help for the boys. This diary was written from 1995/6 up until 2005, while I appreciate a lot has changed since then in regards to the system this is how it was when my boys were born. Although it has been an emotional roller coaster, the boys haven't changed. It was me and my husband Noel who had to change our values, our ideas, and our methods of dealing with negativity. We try not to let it get us down, and we have learned to be very patient with the system.

The caregivers, therapists, educators, special education coordinators, and doctors will provide help for your child, so a word of advice: say what you have to say to them. Be honest, and if it means that your child is labelled as needing assistance badly, then the parents (or guardians) need to get this done. You may want to scream and shout, but that isn't a good idea. You are going to need to work with them, not against them. Be very patient. It has been six and a half years since I first sought a diagnosis for my children. To achieve this, I finally had to go seek private resources.

I should have done this all those years ago, but I suppose I wasn't ready to face anything like this, even though I had my concerns and worries. It's only lately that I've chosen to accept reality . . .

◇ ◇ ◇◇ ◇ ◇◇ ◇ ◇◇ ◇ ◇◇

I don't know how to feel at the moment. Sometimes I am happy and then sometimes I feel sorry for myself. I wonder why my husband isn't as emotional as I am. Then I remember that he is dealing with the issues in his own way.

Did my children get this from the extra drink I had when I was pregnant? Or the cigarettes? Maybe it's because I drank as a teenager? These are only some of the big questions I have pondered recently. When I start thinking this way, I have to remember to stop, that this has nothing to do with my prior actions.

There is a gene called Fragile X that can be tested. Our boys got the test done, but the results were negative. Calm doctors afterwards reassured me that this was good news. "Their disability is not genetic. It's just in the brain." This meant that should my children have kids of their own, they wouldn't pass it on. But I have doubted that statement ever since.

My brother's son was tested for ADHD, and my husband and his nephew are dyslexic. My aunt is epileptic. I have read that when ASD children become teenagers, they can develop epilepsy. Symptoms for dyslexia, ASD, and other certain disorders are very similar. I remember thinking that my brother had ADHD. When young, he was so troublesome, both with the law and within the family. He couldn't read or write adequately and had mitched school when only four years old. Even today, while in his mid-thirties, he struggles with maintaining a safe and healthy relationship, but no matter what we love him very much.

Years ago, situations were different. No one would have recognised that he had any sort of disability or anything similar. People who were like that were put into a home. It was never recognised that there was a hidden disability; instead, it was thought that the cause was a lack of parental affection. It was as if these professionals didn't want to have to deal with children with these types of issues. At the end, these so-called professionals go home. Then we are left with the "what if" or "maybe." Sometimes it seems that these people don't care. Maybe they don't. We never got any feedback on my sons. It was if we didn't have the right to know the doctors' thoughts or their perspectives. I have come to believe that these professionals feel they have to be right before they disclose what they think.

◇◇◇

There is so much to consider when you have special needs children. Take, for instance, hiring home help and babysitters. The first thing you need to do when hiring a professional babysitter is to check the person out. This involves checking references, Garda vetting, and tracking documents. I used to take it for granted that childcare professionals already had Garda clearance when they minded my children—after all, these people are looking after the vulnerable and if they were Garda vetted then how could this have happened? Don't get me wrong, but I know what happened with my family.

My first home help quit after three weeks. She said she was very depressed and couldn't cope. This woman came recommended and qualified. My next helper was an older woman. Please don't think I am age discriminatory, as I'm not.

This helper was told specifically not to lift any of the kids, as they were heavy. I wouldn't attempt to lift them myself, as they weren't babies anymore. The next rule was very important, since the kids tended to run away. I told her to never, ever collect the boys before the taxi arrived. She could only collect them when the taxi stopped and was ready for them to enter. Well, she didn't do any of these things. Instead she collected the boys before the taxi arrived, got into the vehicle, and then gestured for the boys to follow—a very big mistake. The boys, especially my youngest William, instead ran onto a very busy road. The school contacted me about the event. They said it gave them a big fright.

I had rules for a reason. It took me weeks to get the lads to cooperate. There were no sweets permitted for long journeys, as it would make the kids sick. The boys couldn't sleep during the day for long, because they wouldn't sleep easily during the night. When I was informed of the incident where William ran into the road, I reported it to the services. They responded that they would talk to the woman. But I felt so frustrated that she jeopardised my rules, putting the lives of my kids in danger, and I didn't want her to work with my children any longer.

The services took its time in discussing the situation with the assistant. We were worried sick. I rang the boss and told her that I didn't want the assistant working in my home anymore. Eventually, the woman was moved to another family. Meanwhile, my assistant hours were extended from seven hours onwards to thirty hours. Our final assistant would help get the kids home in the taxi, then take William to playgroup, and then provide care a couple of hours in the home. However, she was depressed, suicidal, and untrustworthy. My youngest tried to strangle and bite her. Instinctively, I knew there was something wrong. Although my son couldn't talk, he would point to this woman and scream. I was furious when I was informed that she smacked my child in reaction to his behaviour. When I told her boss, I was further miffed, as they didn't respond quick enough and the woman continued to insist that she was in charge.

This assistant later rang my house explaining the incident by saying that her husband had struck her and that she was taking tablets to cope. Now who was helping whom? I was so worried for the safety of my children. My sister suggested installing a secret camera to record events in the home. I considered reporting the incident to the guards, but I feared upsetting the people who were going to help my children and ending up with no help at all.

I thought there was enough difficulty in my life without asking for more, so I sacked the assistant from my home. The abuse from her husband was terrifying. He called the kids horrible names and behaved like an animal. I even speculated that he might stalk my family just to scare us. I felt that the services had let me down again.

I had put my trust in these people, especially with my children. The services said they would deal with it, but they didn't. I had to do their dirty work. I was relieved, however, when I knew the assistant was gone for good. I was worried sick about reporting this woman to the services, but my mum reminded me that I had enough to worry about. Besides, I would have to be very careful if I were to proceed with anything like that, as I would need proof. Otherwise, it would be her word against mine.

I became very dubious about who my children stayed with. Needless to say, I let the services deal with this woman on their own end. On my side, I told them I sacked her, they knew why, and we declined any more help afterwards. Soon, we received a letter of apology. It said that they appreciated how we had dealt with the situation and they regretted letting the woman's problems be imposed into our lives.

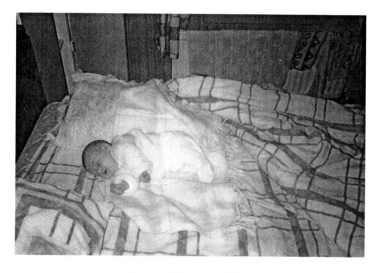

Above: Michael 1 Day

Below: Thomas 1 Month

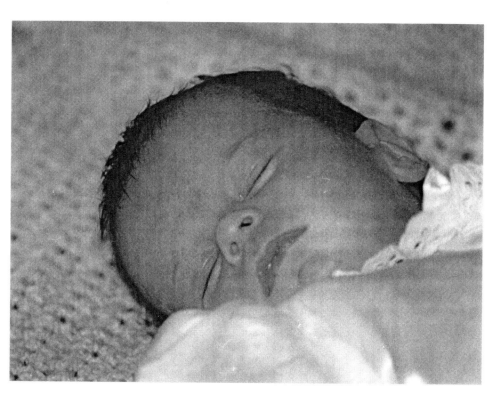

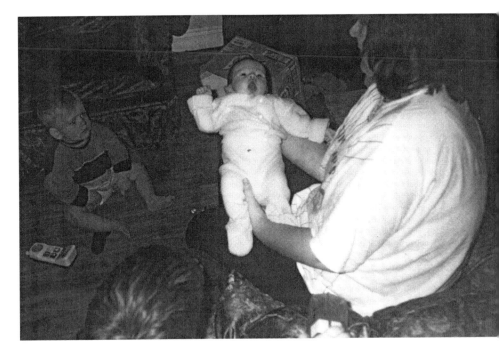

Will 1, Mick 2, Thomas 3

Thomas 3, Mick 2, Will 1

Chapter 2

Let me tell you about my family. I will first go through the pregnancy and birth information for every child, as this is information that the doctors will ask for if you seek help.

Thomas Carey: Thomas was induced two days before his due date, as doctors thought he was small, stressed out, and had a big head. During my pregnancy I felt fine and only experienced some mild high blood pressure. Thomas was born 27 April 1995, after a long labour, and weighed 6 lb. 11 oz. He was breastfed for six months.

When he was young, Thomas was quite an adorable child. He was into everything. He had jet black hair and was a healthy weight. He seemed to be a demanding child, but because he was my first child and a boy, I thought his behaviour was normal. We discovered that Thomas had a lack of hearing in his left ear at eight months, which services nurses said was probably due to him teething. They also said his constant crying was probably due to my jumping at his every whinge. Thomas was able to climb out of his cot at eleven months, got his first tooth at a year, and walked at thirteen months. I don't remember him crawling forwards, only backwards. Thomas was into everything, climbing everywhere, lining up cars in a row, and obsessed with anything having to do with the human body and with nature programmes.

The most unusual things I noticed him doing in these early years included putting stones up his nose and into his ears, and spreading his faeces from his nappy onto the walls, windows, or both. He would also spend hours lining his cars up. I thought that some of his behaviour was odd, but the services made me feel that he was as normally behaved as any other child. Thomas wasn't speaking very clear, so it was suggested that the specialist Sister Imelda examine him. She discovered that he needed grommets in his ears, and she also said that this might eliminate his tantrums, but as time would tell, it didn't.

At the age of one and a half, Thomas had a new edition to the family, a brother called Michael. I though Thomas was very jealous of his brother, as he wouldn't talk to me or hug me much already, and it was worse when I brought home this new member to the family. But he took to his dad, so I thought he simply wasn't very impressed with me.

At around age of two, Thomas got gastroenteritis and had to be quarantined in the hospital. The week leading up to his hospitalisation was the beginning of me losing faith in doctors and hospitals. Thomas was really sick, getting sicker, with watery diarrhoea and zero energy, just lying around. I brought him to our GP who suggested I give him sachets and spoonful of fluids. He threw these up, too. He was getting worse; everything was getting worse. I brought him back to the doctor, but she said I was just panicking and the child would be fine. I was sobbing, as Thomas was clearly doing very poorly.

The next day Thomas was worse, throwing up on an empty stomach. I rang the doctor and asked her to come out for a house visit. She said she was too busy and I was worried over nothing. She said to keep trying the spoonful of fluids and he would be fine in a couple of days. When Noel came home from work and saw how bad Thomas was, we rushed straight to the hospital.

The nurses and doctors were very helpful. They immediately put him onto a drip, as he was very dehydrated, and said he would have to be quarantined in hospital for quite some time. That night, while Noel was at home with our new baby Michael, our doctor rang. Noel told her Thomas was rushed to hospital, to which she replied that was probably the best thing to do.

Two weeks later, Thomas recovered in hospital, but he was so skinny, I couldn't stop crying. My parents thought I was teary because I was so tired, but I couldn't stop crying because I felt my doctor had let me down. I trusted her and she let me down. A couple of months later, I saw her in the shops with a baby. I asked her if the child was hers, and her reply was yes. She shared that although she never planned to have any children, even doctors can make mistakes. That is the truth, but sometimes I think that people think the word "fool" is written on my forehead, as this is the way they treat me. As time moves on, I still get this type of treatment from a lot of people. I don't know why, but it is as if they are looking down their nose at me. But still, I have learned that I have to trust these people even if I don't like them.

Michael Carey: Michael arrived after another normal pregnancy (except for my now usual high blood pressure). I went ten days over my due date, delivery took three and half hours, and he was born weighing 9 lb. 3 oz. Michael was huge and gorgeous. I did try to breastfeed him, but he was a constant crier and always seemed hungry. He was such a beautiful baby, with a gorgeous smile (when he didn't cry). Michael would spend hours on end just sitting there whether he cried or not. He would just play with his hands, and people often marvelled at how happy he was just playing with his hands. Since Michael was always able to find something of great interest in between the tantrums, I didn't think anything was wrong.

As he grew older, Michael showed himself to be a devious child, but he got away with it, as he always looked so innocent. He wasn't easily pleased, and he never wanted to go out to play. He didn't want to mix with anyone; he just wanted to sit around playing with his hands. Today, Michael is afraid of the dark, but as a baby he would sleep for hours. He had most of his teeth at a year and started to walk at one and half years. His speech was very sparse and poor, but the screaming was the worst. He loved to climb on top of cars, into cupboards, and under cars, and to take things apart in seconds just to see how they worked.

Thomas never took to his little brother. All I remember was fighting, crying, screaming, and tantrums. This went on for hours on end, all day every day. I thought that some of the tantrums for Thomas stemmed from the trauma of being in hospital, and then I thought it also might be jealousy, but deep down I had an uneasy feeling that something wasn't right. I was told that it could be the hearing, possibly teething, or maybe it was nothing more than sibling rivalry between brothers. I really was made to feel that I was wasting people's time with these unnecessary worries; they made me feel that I was overreacting.

Michael had constantly swollen tonsils and was always on antibiotics. I put him on the waiting list to be seen by an ENT specialist. One night he had a head cold and he went to bed crying more than usual. I couldn't shift an uneasy feeling; I was really worried about him. I always had the baby monitor on, and on this night it just went quiet, completely quiet. I couldn't hear his breathing on the monitor! I rushed upstairs and took him out of his cot. Instinct told me to put his little chest on my knee and give it a tap. I did, and eventually a bit of phlegm came up. He began breathing, but his tonsils were huge again.

I rang an ambulance, and in the hospital he was put straight onto a nebuliser to help him breathe. Doctors there told me that I did the right thing to refuse his last lot of antibiotics; otherwise, what the doctors in the hospital gave him wouldn't have worked. They said he had recurring tonsillitis because he had become immune to these prescriptions. He was placed on the emergency waiting list for the ENT, and he was treated within two months. In the meantime, Michael had his adenoids and tonsils taken out, and after four days he could go home.

The fighting and the tantrums never eased. If anything, they got worse, but I also put it down to the trauma of Michael being in hospital. If one of the boys eased up throwing a tantrum, my other lad would make up the difference. The only friend the boys had was each other; kids in the neighbourhood just picked on them. There was no way we would have coped as well if we had remained in Dublin. It was obvious early on that our children didn't fit in with other children. We lived in a red light district area, with women doing whatever they wanted with their punters at whatever time. And then there were the kerb crawlers—I was afraid to go walking alone and never if it got dark. I was terrified of what could happen, especially as the kids had no fear of anyone, with no sense of danger. Michael would just go straight up to strangers, hold their hand, and walk off with them.

Shortly after this, I fell pregnant again. As this one wasn't planned, I didn't know how to feel about it.

William Carey: My third pregnancy went well, except for my back. The last week I was myself very unwell—this was a normal pregnancy, but I thought I had a bug. I went into hospital two days before my due date. I wasn't sure if I was in labour; even though this was my third child, I had never experienced anything like this. The pain in my vagina was unreal.

The doctors said I was in labour. I had lost a lot of water, and the doctors said there was very little water around the baby's head. I was having a dry birth, so they put me onto a drip to help improve the baby's movements. Both the baby and I were very tired. Hard labour lasted about two hours, and a vacuum was used in the last push to help bring my child into the world as soon as possible. William was born weighing 9 lb. 4 oz. I didn't attempt to breastfeed; there was no way I could handle this. William was a very happy child.

Chapter 3

◇ ◇ ◇◇ ◇ ◇◇ ◇ ◇◇ ◇ ◇◇

After William was born, the house was just mental and I felt I had no support from anyone, but I'm not joking when I say that I never had any time to pity myself. I had to just get on with things, keep going. On top of everything else, we were house hunting, too. At about five months, William started to scream, cry, and throw tantrums. William's tantrums were worse than his brothers; there seemed to be viciousness in the way he threw his fits. I noticed, though, that William got excited very easy, although I usually couldn't understand what on earth was going on. William had a lovely smile when he wasn't crying. He seemed happy and he made people laugh— he still does.

Sometimes you would hear the boys singing to themselves in their own way, which was so sweet. We couldn't always make out what they were singing, but to hear them in good spirits was heart melting. The boys never rejected any loving, kisses, cuddles, or just playing from us, but if we didn't go to them to play, kiss, and love, they wouldn't be bothered to come to us. I don't even remember any of my kids holding their hands up in the air to be picked up, and honestly this hurts even to this day. I feel that we have been down a very long road with not many positive memories. It is only as the boys have gotten older that they have settled down quite a bit. It is only now that I can say we have happy memories of the past two years and we have had many a good laugh with the boys.

Thomas never seemed to have any problems at the crèche, but when it was time to go or leave, he would cry. The playgroup tutors agreed that there was something not right and reassured me that I wasn't losing my senses. Eventually, with the help of services, I got Thomas into a playgroup. At home, the boys could never play out the front (since in Dublin we lived in the red light district and beside a very busy road). None of the boys understood danger. They tried to go around the corner, onto the road, under cars, and on top of cars, and I would often catch them ringing people's bells or trying to scratch people's cars. I don't think people understood what I was going through; instead, they thought I was a bad mum. I had begun to hate where I lived and feel frustrated with the way the boys behaved. I couldn't leave the kids for one second even to go to the toilet, and no one else seemed to have that problem with their kids.

Thomas, at the age of three years, seemed to be very independent. His screams weren't as bad as Michael's, and I would say he was a bit easier to please than Michael. His favourite programmes on the tele involved anything to do with animals. Thomas and Michael would act like they wanted to kill each other, but other times they did laugh together (what is seldom is usually wonderful). Thomas used to always ram his cars into Michael or to try screaming into his face just to scare him—I never knew why. This seemed to work as Michael used to cry again and cover his ears with his hands in response. Thomas adored William and was very gentle with him. It was like they had this very special connection.

Thomas's tantrums could go on for as long as two hours, but there was no crying or tears—just the screaming and kicking anyone or anything that got in the way. It was very frustrating: I felt sorry for him, but anything I did to please him never worked and just made the situation worse. At three, Thomas spoke quite a bit and could tell me roughly what he wanted or didn't want, usually with the help of pointing and gesturing.

I never asked anyone to mind the boys overnight, as I knew they would be difficult to settle and that no one would sleep. Thomas stayed with my sister once when he was around one, and all he did was cry and scream.

All the boys just loved climbing, and Thomas and William also loved to run, although they had this thing about being in first place and they got very upset if it didn't work out for them. Michael didn't like to do anything energetic except to swim. Thomas occasionally wanted to help push the buggy, which was good as rather than running off at least he was beside me. However, he was adamant about pushing the buggy onto the road and any protests by me led to another tantrum.

None of the boys liked to get their head touched. Thomas didn't like it touched, Michael didn't like it washed, and William didn't like his hair cut. They would let out screams that were just awful, and people would look at me as if I were killing them. There has been a confession to me people thought that my children were spoiled brats because of all the screaming, crying, and tantrums. (Fortunately, now that they have matured, they are much easier to talk to and they have settled down quite a bit). All the boys, for some reason, used to take their shoes and socks off. They all liked to get naked and tiptoe around the place. I used to think they were just into the feeling of being free, and since they were children, I never stopped them.

People said a lot of hurtful things to me about the boys, including: "I think they are a bit backwards," or "You have spoiled them rotten," or "They have you twisted around their little finger," or "There's nothing wrong with those boys—I think it's you who has the problem." Friends would ask me to call up and visit them, since they hadn't seen me in ages, but then they would say, "Eh, don't bring the boys; they're a bit too much. Try to get up on your own." Some people told me I had changed, that I wasn't the same person I used to be.

Any time I questioned any services who would listen to me and hear me out, I was made to feel that I was exaggerating, that I was worried too much over nothing. They attributed it to the boys teething or sickness, or said they were just typical boys and would grow out of it. Some professionals believed they were jealous of each other or probably looking for attention. I really felt I was cracking up, and nobody seemed to know what I was on about.

I knew Michael was going down the same road as Thomas, although he wasn't as energetic. Once Michael got his tonsils out, he didn't sleep as much as he used to and did speak a little better, but he went into himself even more. He had no interest in joining in with play, but I was never too sure if this was because he was quite happy that no one was picking on him for a change. William was going down the same road as well, which was making me really worried. He was still quite a pleasant boy, happy to sit quietly for hours.

Things were very hectic in the house at this stage as the crying, fighting, tantrums, and biting all got worse as the boys grew. And yet the services continued to tell me that it was nothing and that they would grow out of it. Yet they didn't, and other kids noticed and were picking on them, bullying them. The boys went out crying after fighting with each other and then they would come in crying after being bullied outside. It was just never-ending.

Eventually, with the help of services, I got Thomas into a playgroup. It was here they said they thought Thomas wasn't speaking very well. Thank God somebody noticed; I wasn't imagining this. They gave him speech and language therapy every Wednesday, and they said he may have a language problem.

When Thomas started school, I thought that I would enjoy the break with only two boys at home, but it was all too good to be true. The principal at the school asked to see me soon after he started. Apparently, Thomas was very disruptive in his class; he was pinching, kicking, and biting pupils and the teacher. Thomas was also throwing tantrums in the classroom. When he was punished for this and kept in from yard play, he scratched the table. I told the principal that I wasn't happy about finding out there were problems days after it happened; she couldn't punish my child a day later for misbehaving and neither could I.

I learned that when Thomas was kept in from the yard, he had full view of all the other children playing. I told her that Thomas scratching the table was his way of saying he wasn't happy with the way he was being punished. I did think that she was picking on my child. She didn't seem to have experience with dealing with children with extra needs, and she openly admitted that she found him intimidating and she didn't like the way he looked at her. Thomas was four-and-a-half, for God's sake.

Due to his behaviour, Thomas was excluded from school outings and the school never even informed us of any events coming up. It was like they didn't want us to find out and he was being segregated from the other pupils. Thomas couldn't tell me what had happened. Even though he had had speech therapy for the past year or so, communication and understanding was still very poor. As his parents, we had to seek answers and investigate situations. From observing the class and asking pupils questions, we found out that other pupils were bullying Thomas. When I reported it to the principal, she dismissed it, saying she would look into it, but it continued to happen on a regular basis. I wasn't sure how much my son was actually misbehaving, but the older pupils said his teacher and other pupils picked on him daily.

Thomas never got a certificate in school for best attendance, even though he never missed a day. Obviously, he didn't get a certificate for best behaviour. All the other children in his class got something except for him. All the times I collected him from school he looked so sad, as if he were fighting back the tears. Thomas asked why people didn't like him and why they picked on him. As his parents, we couldn't understand why any of this happened or was allowed to happen. I will never forget the tears in his eyes.

I was desperate for answers and decided I was going to take Thomas out of school and report the principal to the Board of Education, while also getting an assessment by the Dublin Hospital. This process, as we discovered, was painfully slow and frustrating, and my patience began to run thin. The Dublin Hospital thought that Thomas had some sort of language disorder and that all the tantrums he threw were part of his frustration. They said they would talk to the principal and tell her they thought that she was being too hard on Thomas and that he was having major difficulties understanding what was been requested from him. Then, as we were finally moving forward, we were told the principal was stepping down from her position and I decided not to pursue my complaint about her.

The woman at Dublin Hospital who had seen Thomas assessed Michael, too. My main concerns were that Michael seemed different, as he was so much into his own company. After the assessments, we played the waiting game again. The therapists did agree that Michael too had a language disorder, and again they attributed his unusual behaviours to his frustration. They said that the boys' constant fighting with each other was their only way of letting off some steam and that the tantrums were for the same reason.

William was coming up on two years of age and he didn't speak a word. Instead, he was throwing a lot of tantrums and biting a lot, too. All three boys dribbled a lot; I used to have to put two bibs underneath their T-shirts so they wouldn't catch a chest cold. The boys' tantrums got worse, and although I tried to calm them down, other kids would still pick on them because of it. I felt so sorry for the boys, and I knew their differences weren't just in my head. They weren't the same as other children, but I was still baffled as to what it was, and no one could tell me either.

William was always a very picky eater. (Truthfully, he still has to have his food liquefied.) If he didn't have a sense of routine with his food, he wouldn't touch a thing. Everything had to be made a certain way, the table had to be laid out in a certain way, and he had to have the same colour plastic cutlery. William used to get a lot of throat infections, so when he got to see an ENT specialist, they agreed it would be best for William to get his tonsils removed and that this might help him be better able to eat.

When William had his tonsils and adenoids removed, he had to stay in hospital with high blood pressure. He couldn't eat or drink anything. William was in hospital for six days. I had begged the doctors to give me an antibiotic for William just in case of infection, but they declined, stating that when his blood pressure went down he would be going home. I didn't want William to go home yet, as I knew he wasn't well and still wasn't eating or drinking. They said that when I got William home I was to commence his prescription. It was very late when we all finally returned home, so it wasn't until the next morning when I got to the chemist.

The antibiotics didn't seem to be doing any good for William, so I brought him to our local GP here in Navan. You could see in her face that she felt for our child. She said his throat and ear had serious infections and said that the little fellow was in a lot of pain. He was prescribed an antibiotic and suppositories, and although he was improving, he still wouldn't drink. I was desperate to get fluids into him, so swallowing my own tears, I lay him back on my knee, and using all my strength as he struggled, I forced him to take some fluids. In that instant, you could see it in his face. It was like he realised that it wasn't so bad, so he stopped struggling. I then sat him up and praised him while he took a drink himself. To this day, though, he will not eat anything lumpy. If he does, then anything he has eaten previously he will throw up again.

◇◇◇

I found an entry in my diary I wanted to share. Here goes:
10 September 2001
My fears and anxieties in regards to my boys: Michael is five next month and William is four in January. The most vital learning point in a child's life is from birth to five years. Michael is awaiting psychological assessment, and to complete this could take up to three appointments at one appointment per week (this is due to services and is the fastest they can go). So there you have it . . . that's now three weeks gone. Then they want to see the boys together, and then the family as a whole. It will take a couple of weeks to complete a report, and then Michael will start speech and language therapy.

The problem is lack of communication, and we feel that although these people are doing their job, they don't really care. At the end of the day, they can go home and switch off. Therapy will depend on how the boys could be slotted into their busy schedule with a lack of resources. Michael needs therapy urgently; he is in a playgroup for three hours a day. He should be in mainstream for his age, but due to his continuous problems, he is just not ready. If he were to go forward for mainstream, it would only cause more problems for him. I feel that the boys' vital learning years are running out.

Michael is settling down a little better in the playgroup each day. But out the front the boys cannot be left unsupervised. Therefore, they can't go out if I have to make dinners or lunches and so on. I think Michael feels left out, and I don't blame him. He blinks a lot more if he gets stressed out and frustrated, which leads to biting, tantrums, and crying

I have voiced my concerns to services, and they said that basically there is nothing to worry about, as the boys are behind anyway. For example, take Michael: he is five, but he seems to have the language and comprehension of less than a three year old. Yet they still say it's okay, that he will catch up. Did you ever hear such bull in your life? Are they trying to pawn me off for a while, or is it that they just don't care? Perhaps they haven't got a clue as to what they are talking about. They really make you out to be a fool and convince you somehow that they are right—they are the experts after all. In the end, we don't have a choice but to trust them, and that makes me angry because I don't trust them. I am pleasant because I have to be, but I don't trust them—there is a big, big difference there.

I have noticed that Thomas likes to bang his head off the wall or hurt himself deliberately by punching his own head himself. He scratches himself to make himself bleed. I know it's part of frustration for him, but I still worry.

I have been looking at some photos of when the boys were young babies, and I have been noticing how destructive they were. Wallpaper never lasted long on the walls; they would rip it with pleasure. I used to go around with paste trying to fix it, but it just looked ridiculous. The other thing they liked to do was create holes in the walls, so I used posters to cover those holes. They would break anything within seconds, but their climbing was the most dangerous thing they did. I think Thomas was two years old when he climbed onto the roof. We asked him to do it again just to show us how he did it, and he completed it with great ease and confidence.

I remember how the three boys always ate muck and dirt, especially from the back garden or any garden. So we decided to concrete our back garden. This worked for a while until they decided to dig a hole. It quickly went from a couple of millimetres to a couple of feet.

William is four years old in January and he speaks very little. He is in a playgroup for one hour, but he is not settling. He has only had one assessment, but the therapists say he is not preschool so he is not a priority. They say Thomas is doing fine so we can leave him alone and that they want to get Michael sorted. Then we will work on William.

When William loses his temper, he holds his breath until he turns purple, and he fights, screams, bites, and kicks. When I see him doing this, I am very scared, as he wouldn't think twice about hitting his head off something sharp. He has no sense of the danger he puts himself into and anyone around him. The last time he did this, he hit his head off a door, then the floor. I am really concerned about this.

I feel that I don't have enough time in the world to sort all this out, and time is running out. I have met some very nice people whom I feel sincerely wanted to help the boys and then some other people who left because they hadn't the resources to help our boys. Every angle I turn seems to be a dead end. I wonder if I went privately—would things get done more quickly? I am grateful for the times when the services has provided taxis to school and back; they sometimes pay the monthly fees of the Montessori and I have gotten home assistance. I have been told that the services are spending enough money on my family. It was actually suggested that rather than getting occupational equipment for my boys, we use the furniture in our back garden instead.

The days go so quickly and I feel I am cracking up, as time is running out and yet so much has to be done. The boys need help urgently, but I feel that I am the only one who sees that. The services tells me to be patient, that they are going as fast as they can and that we as parents are doing a great job. They are a lovely bunch of people—well, the therapists are anyway. They say they are going as fast as the system will allow them to go. They understand I am frustrated and very worried, but they have given my family a lot of help (their words).

Chapter 4

◇ ◇ ◇◇ ◇ ◇◇ ◇ ◇◇ ◇ ◇◇

When Thomas was six years old, one of our neighbours came down to our house screaming. Her partner was with her, and she had something black in her hand. She was muttering something about Thomas, saying, "Look what he did!" She had a dead cat in her hand; it was as stiff as anything.

Thomas was beside me now, and she screamed that he killed her cat, that Thomas told his friends he killed it. I asked Thomas if this was true, and in one breath he said he did kill it and in the next he said he didn't. I couldn't understand what he was trying to say, then her partner added that Thomas collected frogs so they know he killed the cat.

I couldn't understand what was going on; it was all hectic, very hectic. I knew Thomas loved animals, he always had, and yes, he did collect frogs, bees, and insects. I had tried to explain to him many times that it was cruel to collect insects, as they were probably looking for their families. I asked him if he would like it if it happened to him. I also told him that he had to put the insects back where he got them from. Thomas would argue that he wanted them as pets and he didn't want to set them free. I wasn't that worried, as I think everybody at some stage of their young lives collects some sort of insect.

This woman then pushed the dead cat into Thomas's face, screaming at him, "Look at what you have done—you killed it!" I pushed her away and pulled Thomas behind my back; it was all happening too fast. She tried to do it again, and as I opened my door to push Thomas inside our house, the woman's partner pulled her away. I told this woman that she was never to come down to my house and scare my son like that. I said she had no proof and I would talk to Thomas myself. I then told her to get out of my garden.

When I got inside, I immediately asked Thomas just to give me one answer. I told him not to be afraid, all I wanted was the truth, and it was either yes, he did it, or no, he didn't do it. I knew Thomas's language and comprehension wasn't the greatest, but I genuinely couldn't make out what he was saying and he couldn't understand the seriousness of the situation. To be honest, he was grounded for a week, but it wasn't about the cat. As I explained to Thomas, it was about the importance of the truth. When Noel came home, I explained to him what had happened and that Thomas was grounded, but I told Noel that I genuinely couldn't understand anything Thomas was trying to say to me. Noel suggested that he would go seek out this woman's partner and talk to him calmly without anyone freaking out.

When Noel returned, he said he was sorry but the neighbour had convinced him that Thomas did do it. He said the man said he had caught Thomas throwing pebbles at the cat before, and the neighbour also said again that he knew Thomas collected frogs already, which indicated that Thomas had a cruel nature about him.

I wasn't so convinced Thomas did it, but I wasn't so sure he was innocent either. It was a complete mystery. I knew Thomas loved cats—he kept asking me to get him one. He loved all animals. But on the other hand, I had to face facts that I didn't know the truth. A few days later, I spoke to a girl around the corner after I heard her mention a dead cat in her house. She said that early that morning she noticed this dead cat in her living room and she thought she recognised it as the cat from around the corner. She had said to her husband to get it out of the house, but her dog got it by the scruff of the neck and ran out of the house, and she watched her dog run around the corner with it. I remembered that Thomas wasn't out until the afternoon on that day. I also spoke to other neighbours to see if they noticed anything. It took me two weeks to get to the bottom of it, and it was then that I decided that Thomas didn't do it. I didn't go back up to the woman who was so upset over her cat, although I really wanted to, but since two weeks had passed already I thought it was best not to bring it up again, especially since we all had to live in the one estate.

Thomas hasn't forgotten this woman. It's been three years ago now, and Thomas still won't go near the garden belonging to what he calls the crazy woman. Thomas still tells me constantly that he didn't do it, and he cries when he says it. I think he has been traumatised by having the cat shoved into his face like that and being accused of killing it.

This is only one example of something very serious happening that I've had to sort out. People don't see a boy with a disability; Thomas looks perfectly normal. I felt that this woman didn't care or maybe she didn't understand. There are so many people in this world like that; it is upsetting for everyone, but it happens. I regret the fact that I didn't go back up to this woman and let her know what I had found out, but at the time I thought it wasn't worth the hassle. I cringe every time I see her. I wonder if she feels embarrassed as to how she carried on, but then I tell myself to stop. I have many things I regret in my life, but I have to move on and forget about it. Having children does that to you.

◇ ◇ ◇

When we moved from Dublin, the therapists there said to tell the local services that the boys had had their assessments and that they needed speech and language therapy. I told the sertvices this, but they said that because so much time had lapsed the boys would need to be reassessed again. So they were put back on the waiting list which would be for at least a year and a half.

Let me tell you a little about what happened to me. "Why?" I hear you ask. Well, simply because it's an important part of the puzzle. I went into Dublin Hospital for a simple procedure of getting a varicose vein removed, in the recovery room there were complications. I remember it as if it only happened yesterday. I remember lying on my side, and lots of doctors and nurses were running around me. I could hear them saying things like, "her blood pressure is dropping," "her heart rate is dropping," "we're losing her." I could see the panic in their faces, but I couldn't talk or move. I wanted to say something, but when I tried to talk nothing was coming out. The next day the nurses asked me how was I feeling; if I was ok I would be discharged. Nothing was said to me about the night before, so I thought it was a bad dream.

Anyhow, heading off to home, down the corridor, I saw this woman whom I recognised from my lucid moment and as I was looking at her, she stopped in her tracks and asked me if was I going home. I said, "Sorry, Doctor, but how do I know you?" She said she was one of the doctors there the previous night, when they were trying to get me stable, and she said it was very much touch and go; it was critical and I could have died. So, it wasn't a dream it was real. She said it was very real, and I was to take it easy and look after myself. I was to keep a bandage on my leg at all times and return in ten days for review. If the bandage seeped blood, I was just supposed to put another one over it.

Over the next couple of days, I did what the doctors told me. I remember it was a very hot couple of days and I was freezing, plus the fact that I was dozing in and out of sleep. I didn't think I was sick, but I couldn't understand why I was so cold and having hot sweats. I was a little afraid of sleeping so much because I was at home with the boys on my own. My sister Marie came down after a few days with her hubby to give me a hand with the lads. She never saw the back of my leg but she said one of my legs was a bit more swollen than the other. I told her I was grand and don't be worrying sure I'm due back in the hospital after the weekend for a review.

I'm unsure of what next happened but apparently my eldest son went into my sister and asked her could he talk to her. Marie asked him what was up. Thomas said he saw the bandage on my leg and was mammy okay, and that there was a smell. Marie hopped up and ran to me, asking to have a look at my leg. I was laughing and saying what are you so worried about.

She said, "I told you it looked swollen and Thomas says it's smelly, so I think you should get it checked out by your doctor."

"Fair enough, if it stops you from worrying, then I will go to my doctor."

Still not concerned, I brought Thomas with me to the doctor's surgery room. I was to lay on my belly while she had a look, but I was looking back at what she was doing; you see it was right behind my knee. After she removed the bandage, I saw her nearly puke, and she told me to get Thomas out of there. I was in shock, completely numb. She said it was badly infected and that's why there was a smell. She said she would give me a letter to go back up to Dublin, and that I may need more surgery. She said it was very serious.

My husband came home and looked after the boys, while Maria and Pat drove me to the hospital. They were worried and somehow I wasn't. I was asked fifty questions by the doctors and nurses who were looking after me, and they asked me how come you didn't realise you were so sick. I tried to explain that I have three young boys and you just get on with what you have to do, you don't get time to look after yourself because the house is too mental. My Mam and Dad showed up in no time after I was admitted into hospital. My Dad asked for a look but the doctors had it all wrapped up in a bandage. Even then I was wondering why everyone was making such a fuss over me.

Anyhow, I got second surgery. They had to cut out all the infected area where it had gone black The hole was bigger than a golf ball hole and it was very deep. It was, I think they said, third degree surgery. Post-surgery was again doctors said I was critical and it was touch and go. I was kept in the hospital for nearly two weeks. I had to have my wound cleaned three times a day, and padded from the inside out. I remember when I was in having a shower and the nurse said to me that the padding would be easier to remove and wound cleaned from having a shower, so I said okay, no worries. But lads, the pain of the padding being removed . . . oh my God, I fell to my knees in agony. The nurse said we could stop, but I said, "No, just do it. Get it over with."

When I got home I only needed my wound to be done twice a day, again padded from the inside out, it was horrific, but over time it got less and less and, in six months, I was feeling much better and the wound was healing. Now, getting to the point of the whole story, I was allowed to be discharged from hospital and go home on the stipulation that I would let a nurse come to my home and clean my wound as required. I had no problem with this.

So the home-nurse came up and talked to me about my wound and what she had to do to keep it clean. We chatted away while I lay on my bed on my tummy and she did what she had to do. She met my boys and, I think, on her fourth visit, she said when we are finished here can I talk to you woman to woman. I agreed but thought my wound had gone bad again, but she said it's not that. Myself and the nurse sat together and had a cup of tea; I asked what's up. She said that she noticed that the boys weren't talking as clear as other children of their age. She hoped she wasn't speaking out of turn. I was delighted she picked up on what I have been worried about for so long. She also said they had some unusual behaviour, which I agreed with. I confided a lot of information to her, and she asked me could she go back to the office and relay what she has seen to her colleagues so they would be assessed quicker. She did just that, and low and behold all started to roll into place. Shortly after that, the lads were assessed for speech and language. So the moral of the story is that I am very grateful that I went through such a horrific ordeal, having all surgeries and nearly dying, for without that the home-nurse wouldn't have come out to our home and seen our lads. It is my positive from such a negative.

Thomas had started a special unit speech and language class, and I prayed to God it wasn't too late for him. I had put up with the screaming and tantrums for six years, and they were only getting diagnosed now. Michael and William didn't play much out the front; they were stuck in the back. This bothered all of us, and my kids were frustrated and so was I.

I had noticed that Michael and William were putting a lot of food in their mouth, or they were eating too fast. Sometimes it looked like they were just being greedy. I thought they liked the sensation, but it looked awful, like they couldn't get enough into their mouth. I tried to explain to them about table manners and eating, but they didn't get it, they didn't understand.

It was mentioned at this stage that my children could be autistic, but even after a lot of assessments and ignoring the odd behaviour, they also said it may not be and that they should be assessed again. It was said as simply as that, very matter of fact.

If you cringe at the word "autistic," well, that's the term they used, not me. I was getting used to coming to terms with one thing and then being told something completely different. The Services said they were actually new to all of this and really were only learning. They said a lot more families had moved locally and they simply didn't have the resources to deal with them. This was a discussion between two people, right in front of me, talking to each other when they should have been talking to me. They spoke about my boys as if I wasn't in the room or I couldn't hear them.

This was quickly sorted out, but I still didn't know what was wrong with the boys. I didn't know when the next appointment for assessment was. I didn't know what was next! (If you have concerns about one child, please multiply it by three, and you'll know how I was feeling.)

I then wrote in my diary, "HELP ME TO HELP MY BOYS, PLEASE, PLEASE, PLEASE!!!!"

Chapter5

Now let me tell you about our experiences on holiday. Can you imagine trying to explain to resort reps that your children have a speech and language disability, and they need constant supervision, trying to explain in great detail that their comprehension and language is not good, so if there were an accident or they got lost, they would not be able to say what happened or where they were? We told the reps that if they took their eyes off our children for just one second, they would run off in different directions. Basically, I pleaded with them not to let the boys out of their sight. I thought that when you are on holiday and it mentions a kiddies' club . . . well, it's an attractive package because you think you might get a break. Even for an hour would be nice.

To cut a long story short, I was never comfortable leaving my children with the reps. I took a chance anyway, but I always left word where I could be found should there be any problems. My husband and I never moved off; we always stayed beside the pool. Several times William made it up to the pool. It wouldn't be to join me; he wouldn't even notice that I was there. I would watch him just to see what he would do. He would put his hands into the water and swish it around, and I would then go over to him while leaving Noel beside the pool to keep an eye out for Thomas and Michael in case they had wandered from the club, too.

One afternoon, I decided to keep William with me without bringing him back to the reps, just to see how long it would be before they realised he was gone. I brought William back to our apartment and put on his sunblock, swimming gear, and armbands. (William couldn't swim; none of the lads could swim.) I had William for at least a half-hour, enough time that if he had wandered away from the resort, well, anything could have happened to him. The rep did eventually come up to me panicking. She said William was only gone ten minutes and they couldn't find him. I said that I had had William with me the past half-hour and that I wasn't happy and would be making a complaint.

We ended up making a lot of complaints. On another day when it was raining, our resort rep said that the club was cancelled. As a family, we decided to go out for a walk anyway and we found our rep with other reps and all the children they were looking after. So the bottom line was that she lied, and when she saw us she seemed surprised. Just for the record, we did tell them that due to the boys' disabilities they would need another rep there to supervise. I told them everything, explained everything, recommended everything, and we were told our children would be fine. It was the same typical situation all over again: our boys didn't look like they had a disability, so there can't be too much to look after. That attitude is just completely wrong!

If these people would just be brave enough to say that our children were a bother . . . or maybe it was the opposite, that they thought they looked fine so they were treated like any other child. We ended up taking our children out of the club completely, and we told the reps that when we returned home we would be reporting it. When we complained, it was all denied, their word against ours. There is one thing I cannot stand and that is to be called a liar. I was absolutely devastated.

Last year when we went away with the children, we put them into a club while we went off for something to eat. The reps there were more understanding, or maybe our children were easier to cope with because they weren't there for too long.

◇◇◇

On one occasion on holiday, we lost Michael. It was the same usual thing: one minute he was there and the next he was gone. He got outside the hotel and ran straight across a busy main road. A woman on her balcony saw the whole thing and came down screaming, saying he ran across the road chasing a cat—which is typical of Michael—and then he chased the cat back across the road. Michael, of course, had no idea the wrong he had done, but the panic was terrifying. Across the road there was a big open field: very dry, kind of like a desert. If the cat had kept going ahead, then so would have Michael. You would think that we would have learned our lesson then and not went away ever again, but we did. Two years later we tried again, thinking our boys had matured.

I think people think we are overprotective, and I'll admit that yes we are, but we have our reasons. On our last night of this most recent trip, we said we would go out as a family. (Usually the boys would go to bed, and Noel and I would take turns going out.) We were looking for seating for the five of us, and William wanted to dance with the rep, so we agreed. Then, in one split second, William was gone. Oh my God, such panic. At five years of age, William couldn't talk, he couldn't say where he was or where Mammy was.

We ran around calling William's name while clinging onto our two other children. People at the resort started to help us look for him. There were two pools beside us, which is where I thought William was, and the fear that he possibly had drowned was overwhelming. It was getting dark, and so we searched the pools and people headed off to look on the beach. I ran up and down the apartment blocks by the stairs and by the lift. Lots of people had said how beautiful William was, with his big Irish eyes, and I was paranoid that someone had kidnapped him and was doing awful things to him. I banged on doors, sobbing, shouting out William's name everywhere. Some people just looked at me as if I were from The Exorcist.

Noel searched the arcades and the shops, and the reps joined in. One of the reps used the microphone to call out William's name. I tried to explain to the rep that William wouldn't understand what the man was saying. I felt annoyed, as although the rep was trying to help, I felt he was too calm. The rep said our child was five years old and would be back and would be fine. I wanted to punch him in the face.

Suddenly, a strange man walked towards me holding William's hand. He said he had found William at the back of the arcade, mesmerized by the machines. The man asked William to come with him and William obeyed, automatically holding this strange man's hand.

Luckily for us, this man was genuine. I was very grateful for everyone's help. I held William so tight, kissed and hugged him, and then in pure relief I puked up all over the place. I didn't know how to react: I was panicking and angry with myself that we had lost him and then felt such relief when William was returned safely.

As I already mentioned, on most holidays Noel and I took turns looking after the lads while the other person went out. I personally had no objections, but I did get lonely. I longed for the company of my husband, but I knew Noel needed a break too and maybe more so than me because at home Noel was the

full-time carer. He was what we called the "house husband."
When Noel and I do get the opportunity to go out together, we
have such a laugh. Noel is so funny and he's a great dancer too,
and I do miss that. I think that without a quirky sense of humour,
I probably would have cracked up a long time ago.

To go away as a family costs a fortune, but it's very upsetting
when our children start to act up, are bored within minutes, are
fed up, played up, or just sitting there looking sad. I have made a
promise not to go away again with our lads, as it is too traumatic
for all and costs a lot of money. It is only now a year later that
I understand that all the people around us having fun and being
noisy was just too much stimulation for my children to deal
with. They just couldn't handle all the chaos around them. They
were not being bold or unappreciative, which is what I initially
thought. The noises around them just drove them mad, and the
looks people give us . . . it was enough to drive anyone insane.
We had to constantly watch our children, keeping our eyes on
them at all times.

◇◇◇

Just before Michael got into the Montessori school, I tried
to get him into playgroups. Usually I got phone calls saying
he had thrown a tantrum and the other children were petrified.
Basically, on these occasions, I was to come immediately and
collect him. This upset Michael, and the next day he would say
the word "school" and would cry, but he wouldn't be allowed to
go. Any playgroup I tried, within hours he would end up either
expelled (to put it nicely) or simply not be welcome there.

The ladies in charge did admit that they thought Michael
needed an assistant, which they couldn't provide. They openly
admitted that they couldn't cope with Michael's behaviour, and

they were concerned for the other children. Then there were the other children's parents to be concerned about, as it was the staff who had to deal with parents who did not want their children involved in Michael's tantrums, fighting, crying, or pinching.

Of course, all these people had a point. I would be the same and have the same concerns, and absolutely, these other children needed to be considered. Eventually, we got Michael into a local Montessori. Betty (not her real name) his teacher there, had an assistant. This woman, in my opinion, appeared a lot more professional and therefore experienced. I felt that Michael would be well looked after in this setting; my only concern now was whether Michael would settle for her.

I waited for the dreaded phone call. The first day, I kept saying to myself, "Just wait, it will ring any minute and they will say come and collect your child." But the phone didn't ring and we collected our child at the same time as the other children were being collected. Betty said that Michael was difficult, he did throw his tantrums, but he was brought outside for his time out. She said they would take it day by day and let me know how it was going. Two days passed and no phone calls, but Michael was pinching other pupils, crying, throwing tantrums, and the usual. Betty said she would use behaviour modification with Michael: good incentives and ignoring bad behaviours. She said that when Michael was ready, he would join in himself, and of course, he would have to obey the rules.

This plan was to take things day by day, week by week, and then month by month. It was very difficult for Betty and her staff, I do acknowledge that, and I am very grateful to all of them for giving Michael a chance to let his personality shine through. These people who looked after Michael were very nice and honest people. Through patience, they discovered that Michael loved to sing, dance, and draw. Michael became very close to them and he grew into a much happier child. This was the same Montessori that took William the following year, and they helped him, too. When I win the lotto, I will definitely donate money to their school, as they are fantastic.

◇◇◇

My friend was living in an apartment and I knew she liked animals, so I decided to get her a dog. Although she was delighted with the thought, animals weren't allowed there. I couldn't give the dog back to its owners, so we considered keeping him. I noticed that our children would calm down quite a bit while petting the dog, so we decided then and there that we were going to keep him ourselves. The previous dog's owner called him Okie, so we kept the same name.

Okie is a lovely dog, and he is very patient with our children. I think the dog thinks he is human himself. All of our children have pulled Okie's tail, they have wrestled with him, they have chased him around in circles, and not once have I seen Okie snap or growl at them. I believe the dog has taken the children's minds off themselves, and having a pet is very therapeutic. You know the way I mentioned that William wasn't talking properly? Well, the first clear word William ever said was "Okie"!

Chapter**6**

◇ ◇ ◇◇ ◇ ◇◇ ◇ ◇◇ ◇ ◇◇

By April 2004, the boys had been diagnosed with autism. Finally, people were sitting up and paying attention, but it had been nine years since it all started. The next step was to assess the boys so that they could receive the help and support they needed. Although I refused to crack up (my family needed me to be strong), I still cried at night and I still continued to fight for my children's needs. I had met some nice people and some not so nice people. I had lost a lot of friends due to their lack of understanding. But we are all alive and well. Maybe all this misunderstanding stemmed from the fact that the boys looked completely healthy and normal. I still feel that you have to be down and out to receive services, and I think it's easier to get help if your child or children are actually ill looking. My boys were perfectly healthy looking—boys trying to live their lives in their own way.

Services requested that our children need a full occupational assessment and a report. So our boys got a couple of assessments including a house visit so it could be identified what was needed in the home setting. When we got a copy of this report, we were advised to go to the services so that they could help us, which we did. As usual, they had to look into it and get back to us. I was beginning to feel like a nuisance and suspect that they didn't really like our family very much. The therapy person who completed the assessments including the house visit confided in us that he was disgusted as to how we were being treated. He said that in his country if he gave a recommendation report, the family would get what they need there and then, but that was not the case here in Ireland. The therapy person said he would go talk to the Head of Services himself and let us know how he got on.

When we spoke again, he told us that he explained to the Services all about our lads' disabilities. He asked us if there had been any progress with Services providing the necessary equipment for our children, which there hadn't been. This person said that he would give us his honest opinion and that if we ever repeated it to anyone else he would deny it. He thought that if we had one child with a disability and occupational needs, then we would get what we needed, but the fact was that we had three boys with triple the cost. In addition, the Services was currently trying to cut corners, so it was evident that we were going to come across problems.

For example, he recommended that our boys get a table and chairs each separately in their own location. This would help us give our lads individual time outs, it would give them a bit of space from each other, and in time it would help them improve their concentration. The Services, having reviewed this recommendation, suggested that rather than getting a table and chairs each, they could sit together and use the one table and maybe get some bean bags to sit on.

We got a house visit from the Services, and this time there were two staff members who came. They said they were there to let us know what they could do to help the boys with this report. Well, straight away these two women commented that they could see we had a new car (a hire purchase, just for the record). I said that because our children had so many appointments, it was cheaper and more convenient for us to get a car on hire purchase than deal with the expense of taxis. Then I felt I had to explain the TV, which I attributed to the fact we never get out so we liked our home to be comfortable. Since it was a beautiful day, we made our way to our back garden, as William was out there playing anyway. I left my mobile phone on the table, and just for the record, the boys knew not to touch Mammy's phone, so in my opinion it was safe to leave it there.

I told these women from the Services that I had proof that my assistant was suicidal and was sending me disturbing messages. I then left my phone beside the women and headed into the kitchen to put the kettle on to make some tea. When I came back out, I was sick to see one of the women and my child with my phone; they were both doing something with it. Oh, I was horrified and disgusted, I never let any of my children play with my phone and especially now that I had messages as proof that I wanted to show these women—proof of what sort of help I was supposed to be grateful for. I felt I had to prove to these people that I was telling the truth. I took the phone off them, and to my horror and disgust, all the messages were deleted.

I was furious and told the Services woman so. She said she was very sorry and that she saw no harm in William playing with my phone. I replied that there was harm and I told her that I had this proof on my phone that I wanted her to see. I believed the assistant was in need of some help herself and I didn't need the extra burden of this situation. But these women just carried on as if they didn't care. I thought they deleted these messages on purpose; it was just so convenient that my son was playing with the phone and deleted the messages accidentally. I felt that these women were out to upset me, put me in my place or belittle me, which was working, as I felt bullied. I was very uncomfortable with these people and what they had to say to me in my own home.

In regards to the recommended equipment list from our therapy person, these women decided that rather having to spend a fortune on equipment such as swings, trampoline, and a small playground to help with their motor skills, the table out back, if turned a certain way, could suffice. With the chairs turned upside down, back to front, our children could climb in and around this, and it would save Services from having to spend a fortune. These women appeared quite pleased with themselves for making this decision. I told them I wasn't happy with the idea and that it was downright dangerous for my children.

These women went on to say that the Domiciliary Carers Allowance that our children got every month would be assessed regularly and could be stopped at any time. And although I agreed with this type of monitoring in principle, I had this eerie feeling that they were in some way threatening me. They then went on to say that the Respite Carers Allowance that would be received in June was not for the parents, it was for the children only, and that this too could be stopped at any time. If you read the handbook for people with disabilities, it clearly states that this money can be used however the carer sees fit.

If these people came out to my home to make me feel that my children were not worthy of any help, then they succeeded. I felt as usual like I was begging for help and they weren't even prepared to meet me halfway. Then I got angry with myself for letting myself ask again, as if I should have known that they would say no. But I wasn't asking for help for me; I was asking for my children. I felt that nobody cared or that, being Irish, we had to be really poor to get any help.

◇◇◇

Every year our children have been reassessed to see do they still qualify for the Domiciliary Careers Allowance. This usually takes about fifteen to twenty minutes. This year, I was able to bring the reports I got from Professor Fitzgerald. The doctor doing the reassessment took one look at William's report from the professor, and she was so apologetic that I actually felt sorry for her. It was like she was ashamed that this allowance had to be reviewed under the circumstances. Then she said, "I hope your other two children are okay," while proceeding to read their reports.

When she finished, she looked up at me and seemed so surprised, repeating how sorry she was to hear that our three children had autism. This woman was the first woman within the system whom I felt actually meant what she said. She said she had to confess that she had a bad memory, so if I got another letter to have a review, I would just have to mention to her what diagnosis my children had. My next review appointment shouldn't have to be for another five years.

Chapter 7

◇ ◇ ◇◇ ◇ ◇◇ ◇ ◇◇ ◇ ◇◇

After years of assessments and reassessments, we don't really know any more. Maybe my boys have autism and maybe they don't. It is an endless roller coaster of emotions. I don't understand half of the emotions I get. One person might say that my boys have a diagnosis of a disability, while someone else might say that my boys just have difficulties. One person from Services actually said that they had spent enough money on our family and that there were other kids out there worse than ours.

Three and a half years ago, Services said we could have respite care and that they would look into it for us. Then when I rang and queried about what was the latest update on our request, I got grilled about if I even knew what respite was and what I hoped to gain from it. And yet again, they too would have to look into it for us. We have had a few people come in as home assistance (as discussed earlier), and I just want to say that just because it didn't work out for us doesn't mean it won't work out for you. I felt that I had to be grateful for any assistance although they were older, depressed, and even suicidal, or one assistant gave my youngest son a clatter across the face.

We were told that we were not the bosses of these people and that the Services were in charge. That sentence didn't make any sense to me. Surely to God if someone was to come into my home to assist me with my family, then I have every right to be in charge of them and what goes on in my home.

We eventually got our children assessed privately, and I would recommend this to anyone who needs answers. We should have done it years ago. The professor sent a report to us as a family and copied the same to my doctor, who in turn sent a letter of referral to local Services. Local Services has been in touch to assess the boys individually, as they have individual needs. It has been as simple as that and everybody has been very nice and helpful to us.

Today, Thomas is nine years old, Michael is seven, and William is six. All my children have lovely manners. Thomas and Michael have completed two years in speech and language therapy classes, and William has another year to go. It is now confirmed that my boys have a diagnosis of autism spectrum disorder, and Thomas and William also have secondary ADHD and Michael has secondary ADD.

Now that we finally have some answers, there is a little part of us as parents that can relax. It is the not knowing what is wrong that is the killer. I have spent seven years asking questions. I thought I was going crazy, but now I know I am not and that the autism services are going to help our children. For the first time in a very long time, I have a smile on my face. We have been at rock bottom for a long time, and now we are on the way back up with a positive outlook on reality, and it is a good feeling.

◇◇◇

Thomas is very good at Irish dancing, maths, reading, and drawing. His teacher says he is very talented and sometimes he helps other children in his class. Thomas says himself that he doesn't pay attention in class, either because the work is too hard or too easy, or he simply doesn't understand what has been said. Thomas also needs to be up at the front of the classroom so he can concentrate better. Thomas is very good and fast on his toes, but his downside is his forgetfulness and being so gullible. His mood swings lasts for hours (he is either very happy or very sad), and everything he does has to be perfect.

Thomas won an award for writing a book and got a certificate from children's book author Don Conroy. He also got an award for drawing a Christmas picture, which was made into Christmas cards and sold. Academically, Thomas is doing very well, but socially he isn't as good because he has poor social skills. He also still wets himself. Thomas loses friends so easily. If he plays with lads of his own age, the other lads usually try to make a fool out of him or bully him. Thomas questions his own abilities and has poor confidence. When Thomas gets very depressed, he says that he is different and he questions why other children have been so bad towards him. Thomas knows himself—he is a little different.

Michael's speech is fantastic; he whinges so easily, though. Michael is so underactive in comparison to his brothers. What really worries me about Michael is that he just doesn't seem bothered about interacting with others. Instead, he plays with objects or with his hands held up to his eyes. Michael likes to spin on swings, and he hasn't got a clue when it comes to danger or strangers. He will touch people's face, hold their hands. He also likes to either climb onto cars or get under them, whether or not the engine is on. Michael walks on his tippy-toes, and his favourite toy to this day is dinosaurs. When Michael and William are on swings, they have to be closely monitored as they don't swing up and back, they like to twist the rope.

William is doing a lot better now—at least the biting has eased up. The crying is still there, and at school he has had three yellow cards for misbehaviour. If he gets one more, he will be suspended from school. William knows that getting a yellow card is not good, so he experiences panic attacks, which can last as long as a week. With this, William usually gets sick regularly and refuses to eat or drink. William will cling onto me more than usual when he takes these attacks. For a child who cannot tell you how he is feeling and why he's feeling that way, I suppose this is his way of letting me know that he is worried or unhappy about something. It is heart-breaking when he takes these attacks. People have said to me that when William is hungry enough he will eat for me, but he doesn't and is very stubborn. William will only come around when he is ready.

William's speech is improving all the time, and Noel himself has completed the Hanen programme, which has helped us both to understand our children a lot better. When Noel attended the Hanen programme, he was told that he himself could teach the tutors a thing or two, as we probably know more than they do. Some people have asked Noel and me for advice. After completing the programme, Noel received a certificate and he was asked would he come back and give a speech at the beginning of the next Hanen programme. Every year so far seems to get better for our children as long as they continuously get the help and support that they need.

◇◇◇

When I was told that Thomas, Michael, and William all had a speech and language disability, it was at this time when the possibility of autism was dismissed. I felt there was no support or support groups for kids with this type of disability and their families, so I tried to set up my own group called PCSLD, which means "Peers of Children with Speech and Language

Disabilities." I placed an ad in our local paper asking people in the same boat to get together so we could support each other, and in a group we would have more strength to tackle the system. I provided my name and address, but sadly there was only one letter of reply.

It is quite possible that other people out there feel the same way I did at the beginning: maybe they don't want to face reality, and maybe they are not ready to talk yet. I can understand that, and to be honest, I don't talk about it much, only selectively, as I am not ready. This is why I have been recording my thoughts these days, as it's my way of getting stuff off my chest. It my way of opening up and letting my emotions out.

We could really have used the support when we were getting our children assessed for the language class. If you are not familiar with these proceedings, there are a limited amount of places for any language class and hundreds of children enrolling for them. These places are only accommodated based on priority, so although you may think your child is bad, he or she may not get a placement within the class. I remember talking to a woman there who told me about her child and the years of frustration they had been through. She was crying, and I was trying to console her. I explained to her that most children with speech and language disabilities usually recover over time with help, therapy, and support.

I believed this, as Thomas was in a language class and was doing so well. Even at this stage, my husband and I were blind as to the truth. Services had convinced us that it was speech and language problems our children had and nothing else, even though I always had my doubts. I even had myself convinced that whatever the boys had was curable (although I have read that with very mild forms of autism, the child can grow out of it). Now after years of pushing and pushing for our children to experience normal everyday situations with their peers, adults, and friends, they are finding it very difficult to do this as they get older. Communication is still difficult for them, and so they learn to cope in their own way.

◇◇◇

None of the boys likes any change of routine. They hate small spaces and waiting. You have to explain to them constantly what is happening next; otherwise, they become very fidgety and anxious. Our lads can never sit still at home: their bodies are always fidgety or they are playing with their faces or fingers. The boys have improved a lot in school since they got the one-to-one assistance, and the smaller class room setting helps, too. Otherwise, there are too many distractions and problems for them to contend with. But since Noel became full-time carer in December 2001, everything has improved all around.

Thomas loves football lately, and he has been collecting the stickers. We encourage this, as it helps him to mix with others. If you watch Thomas playing football, he loves to be in goal and will literally tumble to save the ball. Thomas worries constantly about the world, tragedies, death, and disasters. Sometimes he will complain of cramps in his tummy; he has had this complaint since he was first able to talk. Doctors have examined him and concluded that there is nothing physically wrong with him. It seems to be part of the makeup of his autism and the fact that he worries too much. The cramps may also be part of Thomas's everyday diet; apparently, those under the umbrella usually thrive better on a gluten-free diet.

Michael is very good at ballet dancing these days. He seems to like the sensation of being on his toes, and his runners only last a maximum of two weeks before the toes get destroyed.

Michael's balance is not great. At the age of seven, he still prefers to be on his own, and he hasn't changed in regards to crying and telling lies. Other children call him a baby or a freak. Michael's best friend at the moment is William. I have watched them, and they constantly like to flap their hands and walk like dinosaurs on their toes. Thomas will join in too but not as much. All three of our boys love anything to do with computers, games, and Game Boys.

William has improved a great deal. He speaks a lot more and he hasn't bitten anyone in a while. Although William talks more, there is still a lot we don't understand. But usually William will lead us to where he wants us to go and he will point to what he wants.

On a personal note, it is difficult to write about the negative side to our children's behaviour, especially when I love my children so much. I have beautiful, well-mannered children. They have had it worse than most folks, I believe, because they were punished for negative behaviour they didn't even understand themselves—and I would bet you that they weren't even aware of it either. Things are more settled now and we can be a family. I will never make up for lost time on assessments or "what ifs" or "maybes," but our boys are healthy and happier. It has been a very long struggle for all of us for years. But what our children lack in one area, they make up for it in another. For instance, they are very visual.

This entire ordeal has been a very hard on all the family. We have had to fight for a lot for our kids and their rights, especially in regards to services. I believe there has definitely been a lack of support and answers. We are now slowly getting answers, and we have learned to support each other. This journey as we know it isn't over yet, and it has been very long, rough, and emotional. If we as a family were still waiting around for the help and support that was promised to us years ago, through sheer frustration with the system I think I would have walked out on my family by now. I was very angry and it literally made me very sick, but somehow one day I was able to take a deep breath, step back, and look at the situation.

We decided to tell Services that we didn't want assistants anymore unless the person would be there to give one of our children one-to-one attention. I told the services manager at that time that as hectic as our children were, we could deal with them better without the stress of having to deal with the Services as well. Now I love my family, and I adore and cherish my children. We understand each other a lot better now. Through sheer frustration, as you know, we went privately to see a professor who authored a book I found in the library called Autism 2000, Breaking Though the Wall: An Introductory Guide to Treatments, Therapies, Teaching Methods, Tax and Welfare Entitlements (O'Grady and O'Grady). At the back of the book are contacts for many people, so if you need additional information, you should check it out.

We have been communicating with the special needs services and they say to be patient with them as they continue to help us with our three boys. I happen to like these people, maybe because I am finally speaking with someone who understands where I am coming from. We have been told that it is not unusual for children with speech and language difficulties to have autism. Just so you know in regards to politics, language disorders and autism are dealt with differently.

◇◇◇

I have just found out that none of my children have an assistant travelling on the local bus, and they don't get met from the bus either. I have been in contact with the principal, who in my opinion seems to have the attitude that unless our children are wheelchair bound, they won't be met from the bus. I got the impression that the principal was saying to me that if I was worried about it that much, then maybe I should be their assistant. He said that he had tried to advertise in the past year with no response, and he asked me if I knew someone or would I be interested in doing a couple of hours myself—as if I don't have enough running around to do anyway. I did think about bringing my own children to school myself.

We had been talking to a TD, and he mentioned that as far as he was aware, our children were entitled to a computer, and yet no one else had mentioned this to me. I had to find out how to go about getting one. I asked the services and the CIC, and they didn't know. I decided to write to our local political councellor and I even rang her, but she never even replied to my letter.

In fact, I never got a reply to any of my phone calls or any of my letters, so I decided to ring the Department of Education. I explained my situation and they knew exactly what I was talking about. They said they would send me out an application for each of our children, but the principal of the boys' school had to complete them too and, like everything else, it would take time for these applications to be processed.

What do you think of this, folks? When I filled out the part that goes to our children's school, I wrote down that our children have autism. The principal rang me to apologise that he never knew that my children have autism, and then he told me he didn't know much about autism either. The principal was curious as to where I got these applications, as the usual protocol was to get them through the schools. He asked me the name and address of my contact. I felt kind of threatened, as he said he was going to speak to my contact, as if to check out my boys' rights and entitlements. Needless to say, we expected this, as the professor had warned us about the politics. Unfortunately, the principal wouldn't sign the application form, since I need a recent psychological report and the last time this was done was three years ago. I replied, "Okay, fair enough." Then he said that if William has "this autism," he is in the wrong placement and he shouldn't be in the language class.

Noel says I am like a Pit Bull dog (nothing to do with my looks) with a bone in my mouth, and I just won't let go. He says that over the years he has seen my tears, my anger, my frustration, and all the moaning and begging I have had to do, but I never gave in. Noel says that we should never expect anything from anyone and that way we will never be disappointed. The fact that I never gave up looking for answers and services—I think that is why I am not liked by many people in the services, but so what? With certain people, the feeling is mutual, but again lads, "don't shit on your own doorstep." You have to be smart and remember that while you may not need this person's help now, you may need it sometime in the future.

Chapter 8

◇ ◇ ◇◇ ◇ ◇◇ ◇ ◇◇ ◇ ◇◇

Now let me fill you in on what is happening at the moment. Recently, we had an appointment with the special needs services. They requested to see our children for an informal play assessment together; our children were in one room, and Noel and I were in another room discussing our children with another member of the team. We were asked what we wanted for our boys and what we wanted for ourselves. We replied that if they agreed with the professor that our children have autism, even if it is only a mild level, then we want them to "label" our children.

You see, if you don't label your child as having whatever disability, then your child could go through his or her early life without any help whatsoever. We had spent too many years fighting for our family to get any recognition or help. I hoped that because our children had matured and were receiving the present help from the services, that this would make up for all those lost vital years and our children would blossom to the best of their abilities.

After this initial appointment, Thomas had his first appointment without his brothers to assess his needs. Since I wasn't in the room, I only know what Thomas relayed to me. One assessment, I think, had to do with memory, and another looked at Thomas's speed of recalling details, shapes, and colours. From these assessments, we were advised that it was only a prognosis, and a report would be written out at a later date. The same assessment process applied to our other two children.

It was the special needs services' opinion that Thomas did indeed like a challenge, and the fact that he was extremely challenging with us as his parents did not mean he was naughty but that he enjoyed the sensation of a challenge—it was a sensory issue for him. They said that they would help us teach Thomas about his social issues and guide us in discussing with him why he is different from other children. We would then hook up with the other members of the services team, and Thomas and Michael would be assessed at least two more times (one of these assessments would be done at our children's school). Then at the end of the month, we would discuss all the information we had gathered in regards to our children and how it would be best to meet their needs.

It was suggested at a meeting for Michael that he had the typical "textbook" autism. They told us that our children would never follow in our footsteps, as they had their own values and ideas. All we could do was to try and channel their talents so we can work to develop their positive side. For William, they didn't think we should label him just yet, as he was doing so well in the language class setting and it would be best if he could complete another year. Then, when he had completed his second year, he would be reassessed to evaluate his updated needs.

A week later, we had a parent–teacher meeting for William with a member of the special needs services team present. It seemed that William had indeed progressed well. However, although he was six years old, any initial services assessments tried on William were unsuccessful, as he just would not cooperate. They said it wasn't that he wouldn't; it was because he couldn't. It was obvious that William didn't like being in the company of too many children, as he could not cope with this type of environment. They had been segregating him into a smaller yard, and because of this his behaviour had improved. Even when William returned to his class, he was not as frustrated as he used to be. William seemed to have eased up a little on his pinching of other children and being aggressive, although at home he hadn't at all. William still had the tendency to hurt any child who did better than him in any way.

William's strengths seemed to be in maths and colouring. There was a senior class mixed in with William's junior class, and the teacher was surprised to hear William answer some of the questions not intended for his level. William was being integrated into another classroom for a short period of time, and he had improved there, too. He was learning to take turns and had learned to put his hand up if he had something to say. William still had a very short span of attention and needed coaching and eye contact to return to the teaching situation.

From all the assessments that have been completed recently, it has been discovered that William's comprehension and language is that of a three year old, even though he is now six years and seven months old. At home, William was still unable to ask for a spoon, plate, or even food. Initially, William liked to wander around, get under tables or climb over them, and if he was asked to sit down or to cooperate, he would throw a tantrum. William now gets time out, and this helps to calm him down. William, as mentioned, is very visual, so these areas have been maximised to support his deficits in regards to auditory processing.

William would like to do tasks of his choice, which obviously runs against daily planning and/or instruction. But all of us as a team are monitoring William's behaviour and he is encouraged through positive responses. Visual prompts are very useful and helpful, leading to better cooperation and overall behaviour.

William has improved with his listening, attention control, communication skills, and expression of language, and he is a child who is very keen and anxious to learn. In addition, William is now able to hold his pencil, although his penmanship skills are poor.

Obviously, hearing all this was very upsetting for us as parents, as we didn't think William was that bad. We knew he was a jolly fellow and indeed very clever, and I felt I was right about him not getting help all along. I felt that we would all need to work very hard, including William, to improve the situation a great deal for him. William would need to learn social skills as well. But looking on the bright side, it was all progress. The problem had been acknowledged, and William would get the help he needed. We decided that it would be a good idea for William to complete another year in the language class. It was not easy to get the authorities to agree to this, but thankfully this time they did.

If you think you are right about your child and there is a problem with him or her, whether physically or mentally, trust your instincts and go with it. If you depend on others to give you answers, based on my experience, you will be left waiting.

◇◇◇

With Michael's parent–teacher meeting, it was obvious that he had a problem. They said that if we thought Michael was fine in his own world that he retreated into, then we were wrong. They felt that Michael was going more and more into himself and that it was possible that Michael was at the stage that he was questioning himself: why he is different and why he is not getting honest answers that he can understand. They believed this was causing Michael to withdraw into his own world even more. They said the worry here is that if the withdrawal occurs to the extent that Michael becomes lost within his own world, we may never get him back to reality.

At the meeting, they reported that Michael's work was declining, and it was obvious that he needed structure and routine. They said that when Michael does things out of routine or character, it suggests that he doesn't understand or comprehend reality. Apparently, Michael does his daily routine out of habit. For example, take the summer holidays, or any holidays, which are very tough for our children. Michael especially will be put out, and anything he has learned over the past couple of months, I am told, will be forgotten by him. They also said that although Michael lies a lot, he is not aware that he is telling lies. Apparently, Michael is saying what he thinks is what we want to hear.

They told us that we would have to keep a constant eye on Michael. They also pointed out that Michael still tends to intrude on other people's personal space. We have noticed this and that this annoys a lot of people, including adults, but Michael is not even aware that he is annoying anyone and then he wonders why other children won't play with him. They told us it would be another week before we knew exactly what school placement is best for Michael. It is agreed that he definitely needs a full-time assistant and extra tutoring. Michael's initial services recommended that Michael go into mainstream school with support, but the special needs Services people were not confident that this was right for Michael. They thought he might need to go to a special school for autism.

At this meeting, Michael's teacher Linda (not her real name) asked Noel and me how we were. Obviously, we didn't answer straightaway; we just looked at each other and then eventually replied together that there was no "us" and that the five of us were one team. Linda walked with us to the door. She is from Australia and she is lovely. Linda explained that she meant no harm when she asked us how we were; she said she was just concerned. Noel and I explained that it was fine to ask us; it was just that she was the first to ever ask. We said that we had been down a difficult road with our children and help hadn't been easy to get. Linda agreed and said that although there was a lot of negative stuff said in regard to Michael, the positive side was that he was a lovely child who had autism, which made him different. She said she loved Michael and would like to teach him for longer, but unfortunately she had to return home at the end of the term. I don't know how many times I fought the tears over the years, but as I looked into Linda's eyes, I saw she had tears in her eyes, too. Linda is a genuinely caring person and she will be missed, especially by Michael.

In all honesty, I have to agree with the special needs services, as Noel and I feel that if Michael were to go to mainstream classes, even with support, there is no way he would survive. And we also believe there is no way that a teacher would notice a child slacking off severely with a full class to control. We are still afraid to admit this to anyone, so we are reluctant to say anything. But we are also terrified that we may make the wrong choice for Michael, since he has been through so much already. But we have to make a choice and pray to God we are doing the right thing for him.

We are like piggy in the middle between the school and the services. We are not experts, we are just parents, and as parents we feel Michael will not survive in a mainstream classroom setting—he might in a couple of years, but definitely not now. We have decided this and now we just have to tell the school. When I left the meeting, I was absolutely distraught, trying to fight the tears; even though I wasn't sobbing, the tears were rolling down my face. Noel told me that if I wanted to cry I should just let it out, but I felt I had to be strong.

◇◇◇

The situation with our children has never changed; it is no different to what we are used to. But for us as parents, it is our attitude that will have to change. I am very angry. We expected that our children had problems but not to this extent. How in God's name did our children get all these assessments over the years and nobody picked up on what I was talking about? Is it just that these people were thick or ignorant, or maybe, as I have mentioned before, they go home at the end of the day and they don't care?

I have to keep myself and my mind busy in order for me not to crack up. Please don't get me wrong: I don't feel sorry for myself, although it probably sounds like it. I feel it for my boys and all the crap they have had to go through over the years when no one believed me that they were different and were having problems—no one, that is, until I met Professor Fitzgerald. To him I would like to say a big thank-you. He saw our children and wrote a report of his assessment and conclusions, and hence opened a can of worms that everyone else chose to ignore. Trust me, it wasn't about the money. Yes, the professor was just doing his job, but he was very charitable and the fees were what I could afford. So there are nice people out there, and I am seeing this lately. I still get very angry and upset, but when I look at my boys who are oblivious to what is going on, I fight my tears and come back to reality.

Thomas had an appointment again today with the special needs services. At this point, my children are going to go to different schools due to their different needs. The services people thought this was best too, as it would ease the competitiveness between the brothers. They requested to see him again next week, and then we could sit down the next day to discuss everything we have discovered about all my boys and how it would be best to help them. I simply said that we may not like what we are told, but we need to know everything and we need to tap into what they are best at and encourage that so all is positive all around. I have not got a clue why the special needs services does the assessments they do, even though it has been explained briefly. But they are the experts I have to depend on, and again, I have to put my faith in someone for my children's sake.

The past couple of days have been very hard to deal with, but last week I was devastated and couldn't even look at another person for fear of bursting into tears. This week I am starting to tell people about my children, even though I am still very emotional. I have been having this nasty realistic dream every night that involves my children and water in some way. My boys in my dreams drown, and although I am around, there is absolutely nothing I can do about it to help or save them. It is totally out of my control. I wake up sweating and breathless, as in my dreams I have tried my best to help them but I can't. It overwhelms me, leaving me exhausted and emotional.

Noel reckons this all has to do with the news and information about our children we have been getting recently. The fact is, they have autism and there is absolutely nothing I can do about it. It is totally out of my control. We are hoping to get advice from the special needs services as to how we can help our children or how we can understand them better. They are to tell us what assessments they have done with them, what it means to them, and what they are going to do to help our boys.

These assessments didn't take that long to complete—not as long as any other assessment our boys have had. I have mixed feelings about this. I am still very angry and upset with the system, as to how they could have missed something as important as this. I said it before and I will say it again: I knew all along there was something different about our children, as that sort of unusual behaviour was not normal, but I am angry with myself, too, because I believe I was too soft or polite. I never shouted or screamed loud enough without an apology after it. Why was I so soft with these people?

Everyone we met within the system said that Noel and I were a lovely, hard-working couple and that under the circumstances we were doing a great job. Was that their way of telling us to back off a little and to let them get on with their job and stop harassing them? Or were Noel and I so wrapped up with helping the children get their needs met that we forgot how to acknowledge and receive a compliment? I will never know the answer, but as long as I live, I will keep asking myself that question: how did they miss it?

Thomas is nine years old now and I am hoping that we can get some sort of closure to all the nagging questions we have. We cannot handle any more surprises in regards to our children. I really hope that we have heard the worst and from here on in it is going to be better and there will be progress, but time will tell and we shall see.

◇ ◇ ◇

Now, don't get me wrong; I have mentioned Services quite a bit and how much they have let me down. But I am meeting more people lately from special needs, a support worker from the services and others who are genuinely trying to help, and they make up for the nasty people I have had to put up with over the years. They are very helpful, and we appreciate all they have done and all the support they have given us. Up until we met these people, we had lost all faith in anyone working within any services. We don't hate going to meetings as much with these new people. Just to sit with someone who knows exactly how we are feeling and actually wants to help . . . they listen and it makes us feel much better.

Chapter 9

⬦ ⬦ ⬦⬦ ⬦ ⬦⬦ ⬦ ⬦⬦ ⬦ ⬦⬦

I haven't told you about my family's response to this entire situation. I genuinely forget that they too have feelings and get upset as much as I do, especially as they know how hard I have taken the whole situation. My mam and dad have been there for all my family more than 100 percent. If I want to talk, they are there to listen and give advice. I have found it extremely difficult to talk to my family as a group, but one by one I can talk to them individually.

Don't get me wrong, it is not my family who have difficulties expressing feelings—it is me. I thought I was ready to talk without crying, but I am not. I am trying to talk and I am fighting the crying. I am pretending to be strong when obviously I am not. I think Mam is trying to help me face all of this from a realistic point of view by telling me stories of other people who are in worse situations. Even though I know Mam is right, her consoling words don't work. At the end of the day, these children are my boys, my flesh and blood, and for now I just can't seem to see beyond that. Mam says I am a big softie, and she is right (again, at this moment, I am fighting the tears). Mam also says I am a very strong person and very wise, as I never gave up, even after all these years.

My dad has worked with children and adults with all kinds of disabilities, so he has experience in this field. And now that he knows there is a reason for my children's constant misbehaviour. My parents absolutely adore my children. I am not sure if Mam and Dad are finding it extremely difficult to either understand my boys, or maybe, like the rest of us, they are finding it difficult to come to terms with this autism. My father says that Noel and I are a godsend to our children. In all fairness, both my parents are trying really hard to understand our situation.

Dad's health has been up and down, good and bad. When my boys were younger and we would visit we would keep our children outside waiting in the car as they were very hyper. You might think this was really cruel, but remember that Dad's diabetes was very bad and plus he had had many heart attacks. So sending in my children, who were overactive, was not a good idea, since he was trying to recover,

My sister, Debbie, is studying autism; she is starting exams. Debbie is great with my children and so patient with them, and I think she is educating the rest of the family with all that she has learned. Just imagine your child pulling the hair from someone's head and the panic you would feel as to what kind of reactions people would have. One time we as a family went to a christening, and the hall was packed. I was trying to get William to stop having a tantrum—honestly, I was mortified—and Debbie was so casual. She said she was fine and she would deal with it.

Even before I had a diagnosis for my children, Debbie was very supportive, and over the years she too has always agreed with me that my children would meet the criteria for autism. I have had no problem talking to Debbie and telling her what's going on, but what I never got to say was how upset I've been. By God, it is good to talk to someone whom you know in your heart understands. Debbie has said that she has really learned from all the things our family has experienced—things that she could never learn from a book.

My sister Maria is the eldest. She too has been very patient with my children, but she used to panic so easily if any of my children started to cry or get boisterous and noisy. In Maria's defence, the pitch and volume of the noises my children would make were hard on anyone's ears. Maria was always looking out for my children, but she was the hardest to tell about my children's diagnosis. I really had to fight the tears when I was talking to her. I know she feels my pain, but she cannot control her feelings, and if I cried, then she would cry. Don't get me wrong: she has a heart of gold. But her kindness can leave me in tears.

My other sister, Alison, just had a baby recently, and maybe it is wrong of me not to tell her what is happening with our children, but I am leaving that up to my mum. You see, her child is gorgeous, my sister and her partner are so happy with their new baby in their life, and to put it simply, I don't want to ruin that for them. I don't want Alison to worry about my children as well as her own baby. I just want her to have as much fun with her little one, as they grow up so quickly.

My brothers look after me so well, and yet I don't discuss any of this with them. They know my children are hyper, but I don't want my brothers to worry about my family, either. Besides, they are much younger than I am, so I wouldn't expect them to understand what I am going through. I have discussed it with my brother, Michael (my immediate younger brother), and he tries to understand. I explained some of my situation, fighting the tears as usual, and he was very sympathetic towards me, which didn't help the fact that I was doing my best not to cry. He tried to comfort me by saying not to worry, that they would grow out of it. That is when reality set in for me, and I said to my brother that actually the boys wouldn't grow out of it, that it is for life. What I knew in my head didn't sink in until I said it out loud. I also told my brother Michael that even with their autism and ADD/ADHD diagnoses, he didn't have to treat them in any special kind of way. He was to treat them the same way he had always treated them. Micka and Hanna came over many nights to look after the lads for me, they have many fond and funny memories of when the lads were just babies, just as I have many fond and funny memories about them babysitting too.

Joe is Ali's twin brother, Ali and Joe are the babies of the family. The youngest of us 7 so to speak. I have had both coming over and babysitting the lads for me, shortly after this is when Ali became a wonderful mammy herself, then Joe came over on his moped to babysit the lads, then the next day as a way of saying thankyou to Joe and Ali Noel would take them up the phoenix park in our car to teach them how to drive. Again there are many fond and funny memories here. Some are too private for the whole world to read, but they themselves will giggle as they understand.

There has been many a night that my family has helped out either babysitting, giving some words of advice, or sometimes just listening to me babbling away. Everyone in my family has been very good to us in their own way.

One dear friend, whom I had lost contact with over the past years, rang me to see how I was. She has tried to keep in contact with me, but I personally lost interest. Last year this friend wanted me to become more social, but I had no interest as I had been working part-time nights and had not been around for my children. My husband was doing a great job as a full-time carer, but I had to admit that sometimes I felt left out. Plus, we usually had an appointment for one of the boys, or I was working, or we just wanted to chill out at home, go nowhere, and do nothing.

I feel I haven't the energy to explain to friends why I don't bother to ring them, why I don't call up to see them, why I am not in the mood to go for a drink, but I believe that true friends don't need an explanation, they just accept things as they are. I'm just not often in the mood to socialise, and to some extent I feel I am intruding in some way. Although people ask how things are, I feel they get bored listening to me talk about my children.

Sometimes friends would offer to come up to my house. Usually I didn't mind, but there were times when I was too exhausted to entertain, and I felt that if I said this they wouldn't understand and may take it personally. Another friend I lost touch with or didn't bother to make the effort with confronted me, and I tried in vain to explain my situation without bursting into tears. Sometimes I feel people have to see you in tears just to realise how serious you are, but if I could help it, that wasn't me. I refused to break; I really had to be strong. Sometimes I would decide that today was the day that I should make that extra bit of effort, and then I realised I was not ready. I suppose some people may see that as being selfish.

Another friend has been suggesting to me lately not to shut myself out from the world. She keeps telling me that I should talk and get it off my chest. My attitude, right or wrong, is that I will talk when I am ready and especially not when I feel I have to. I know I should talk to someone, but I get fed up so easy with people judging my situation without understanding. This goes on day in and day out, so this is more than likely why I don't bother to socialise anymore.

We have regular appointments with our boys, and it doesn't matter who you have seen the last time, but whoever you get to see this time will ask you the same questions. I feel that I am constantly repeating myself and these people leave me exhausted from answering the same questions over and over again. So when this is over, I don't feel like having a social conversation. Besides, some people give you the body language to say they are not interested anyway. I know I have developed a very selfish attitude, but can you relate to what I am saying?

There is nothing selfish about wanting to be with your family, so it can't be a bad thing. If I do go out socialising, my husband doesn't mind at all. He usually looks after our lads and he will escort me to where I have to go to make sure I get there safely. But when I get to sit down, I feel guilty that I am out having fun and Noel is alone at home. I can never shift the uneasy feeling— it's like you feel that something nasty is going to happen. It takes me awhile to get comfortable, and usually I want to go home. Can you relate to this? As chaotic as the house is, as messy as the rooms are, this is where I am comfortable, this is where it feels good to be myself—this is my home.

Chapter 10

◇ ◇ ◇◇ ◇ ◇◇ ◇ ◇◇ ◇ ◇◇

Homework lately has been a nightmare, trying to get our lads to sit easy for five minutes and concentrate on what they have to do and to try to do the work neatly. They get so irritated so easily, and we have to separate them so they can do their best. If you keep the three of our lads together, they either get aggressive or giddy and nothing gets done. Just picture this, please: one of our lads at the table in the kitchen, one at a table in the sitting room, and the other lad at the end of the sitting room. They are hungry so we give them something to eat. It's getting late, so dinner is being prepared. Then one of our lads says he is stuck with his work, then the other, then the other. God forbid if the phone rings; it drives me mad when people ring and I don't get to answer it for whatever reason but then that person doesn't even leave a message on the answering machine. They then ring again, or a neighbour's child calls in to play.

Now, I know this happens to everyone, but all this chaos makes our children crazy. Usually they get overexcited, then frustrated, and then they can't complete their homework. If our lads don't finish it one night, they have to complete it the next night. Bear in mind that it doesn't matter if you explained the maths to our children already, they probably have forgotten how to do it. And due to a lack of imagination, they get frustrated doing English short stories. The list goes on and on. Friday is a good day, as there is no homework to be done.

Michael's and William's teachers use stickers to encourage good behaviour (which works, by the way). Our lads have to complete a whole card (a sticker a day), and then when this is done, they get a small toy or something to do with animals. When our children come in from school, they are very excited, asking me to guess who was caught being good in school. It is a useful tool to promote good behaviour.

◇◇◇

Today we had the meeting with the special needs services. Three of them came, one of whom was taking notes. I have been very anxious and nervous as to what we would be told, but as Noel reminded me, we can't hear any more bad news. We were hoping we had heard it all, but all the same I was still very concerned. They started with Thomas and what the assessments told them of the difficulties he is having. It seems he is not familiar with the use of simple everyday words, especially within the classroom setting. Thomas doesn't seem to be able to use imagination either. For example, Noel was late collecting Thomas, and the only thing that came into Thomas's head was that Noel was dead, not that the car broke down or that Noel had to get petrol. There is only black and white with Thomas, definitely no grey areas.

We were advised never to be sarcastic towards our children, as they will never understand. They said it is obvious to Thomas that he is different and he knows it. He has Asperger's Syndrome, which comes within the Autism Spectrum Bracket. Thomas lacks confidence with himself, he is very doubtful of his accomplishments, and he is aware of his own feelings, so he will do his best not to draw any attention to himself.

One of the special needs services members went to Thomas's school to see how he was getting on. She was very surprised at what she discovered. She said it was obvious from the assessments that Thomas was having major difficulties with the tasks she had assigned for him, so much so that there were many times when she knew Thomas was going to cry or she noticed him trying to distract her from testing him. She said that he was fully aware that he was being tested and that the limelight was on him and his weak areas were showing.

Thomas didn't like this feeling, so to distract the tester from his weaknesses, Thomas would get cheeky with her. He would refuse to do tasks, or he would start messing around or farting. The assessor was well aware of what Thomas was trying to do, so she took it in steps. She spoke with Thomas's teacher enquiring how he was getting on in school, including the yard. Thomas's teacher said that he wasn't too bad in the yard that he was just too boisterous and sometimes he played on his own.

Academically, Thomas was doing fine and there didn't seem to be any problems. He was within the average range, and she didn't think there were any areas of concern. But the lady from the special needs services wasn't so convinced, so she asked permission to assess Thomas in the classroom and the yard. Thomas teacher obliged, and from the assessments it was discovered that Thomas was having major difficulties. She said to bear in mind that Thomas is very self-conscious, fully aware that he is different, so he does his best not to get noticed. When Thomas has a problem understanding requests (which it's obvious he does), he will not let his teacher or classroom assistant be aware of this. They said that Thomas is very visual: if tasks are shown to him, then he will understand, but without being shown, he literally can't imagine what is meant. This, for Thomas, is a major problem.

She also discovered that the other children are fed up because Thomas constantly looks at their copy to see how the work is done. Once he sees how this is done, he gets on with it and it works out. Thomas's teacher was surprised that Thomas was fooling them; she thought he didn't have any problems. The special needs services said that Thomas will always need help: an assistant just for him and tutoring for social skills, language, comprehension, and empathy skills. These are the areas that Thomas is very weak in.

The help Thomas desperately needs will be set up as soon as possible, probably in September. The special needs services said that we as parents must remember that Thomas has worked extremely hard to keep up with the teacher and it has been very difficult for him in an everyday situation to keep the limelight off himself, to be able to fool his teacher and classroom assistant the way he did. That, in itself, took a lot of hard work.

We were advised to keep the rules very simple with him and that any explanations need to be brief. We can keep Thomas in the school where he is; it seems the school is very proud of how well Thomas is doing and a lot of work has been put in to help Thomas progress within the language class. I am not holding any grudges, but when Thomas was discharged from the language therapy because they said there was no more they could do for him (they told me to just keep an eye on him so he doesn't fall behind), they made me feel that I should take their word for it, that he would be fine. I didn't, as I knew and felt that there were issues not addressed and I was furious that he was discharged so easily. To be fair, I could understand that the language class Thomas attended did do all they could, but to dismiss Thomas and hand me back the report saying to keep an eye on him as there was no more that could be done?

When we got the report from the professor and gave it to Thomas's teacher, she said she had her suspicions and she would speak with Thomas's ex-therapist and get back to us. The following day, Thomas's teacher said that after discussing the report with his ex-speech therapist, there was no more that they could do and they didn't recommend that Thomas should take the Ritalin as suggested.

We didn't want their opinion about the Ritalin; we had made our minds up in regards to that already ourselves. What we wanted to know was what they were going to do to help Thomas in regards to the report and diagnosis. We wanted to know how they were going to meet Thomas's needs. Thank God I didn't just accept their word and followed my instincts. I don't even have a problem with Thomas's teacher. I always thought she was nice and I believe her when she said she had her suspicions. She queried the speech therapist and took her word as valuable, which in my opinion was a big mistake, and let it get the better of her judgement. I would like to say that all of the class teachers and assistants who worked with Thomas, especially within that language class, were very nice.

◇◇◇

Again, they said that Michael is textbook autistic. He stands out from the crowd, and he is less inclined to mix or initiate play. Michael has his own ideas and play. The special needs services said they were aware that the speech therapist from his class was eager for him to start mainstream school and resource teaching, with a full-time assistant. The therapist said that if they can tap into Michael's brain they believe he has high potential and that she would talk to the teacher about Michael getting in mainstream and securing the help he would need. It seems that the speech therapist Michael has at present is optimistic regarding Michael and that is why she is keen that he is placed in mainstream.

We have argued that if Michael is placed in a class of twenty pupils, even with an assistant, he will sink. When Michael has been placed in mainstream in the past, sitting for half-hour periods regularly, he did settle eventually, but he still went into his own world. Michael still likes to be on his own. The teacher of the class Michael was integrated into said that for a couple of minutes per week Michael was not so bad, but it would be a different story if he were in a mainstream setting full time. Then Michael would have major difficulties.

We told the special needs services that we were hoping to get their opinion based on their experience with our children, but as parents our hearts were saying that if Michael went into mainstream with an assistant and resources, we still felt he wouldn't flourish. We said that we were hoping he would get into a special class that would suit his needs. We said some parents didn't like to hear the bad things about their children's needs, and even though we didn't like to hear it, we certainly wouldn't ignore it and we wanted to do all we could for our children.

The special needs services agreed that Michael would be best suited in a special class for autistic children and were hoping we would be successful with our application for placement. It would take a couple of days to a couple of weeks to find a placement for Michael, and that's only if there was one available. They were hopeful and certain they would find Michael a placement, but until they were 100 percent certain, they didn't want to say anything. If Michael did get placed in a special class, it could even start in July, as these classes are set up for children with autism who need routine and structure year-round.

This would not be like every day schooling; it would be more like a summer camp where they draw pictures and go on outings. It would more relaxing. In a special class, the same routine applies as in a mainstream setting, with the same curriculum; the only difference is that there are only five students in the class, with a teacher and an assistant. They said that Michael may have to go to mainstream, but that would only be until there was a placement found for him within a special class.

As with any other school, just because our child gets a placement doesn't mean we will accept it. We will be going to look at these possible schools, talking to his teacher and talking to the principal. After all, you wouldn't just leave your child anywhere without checking it out, right? Again, it has been said that Michael has autism, and the special needs services thinks he is the worst of our three boys and we definitely agree with them. The special needs services says that, like Thomas, Michael has worked very hard at school, although his handwriting is very poor. Michael always tunes out, he puts objects up to his eyes, and he definitely needs visual stimulation, and all of these would be addressed. Michael also needs tutoring with empathy training, social skills, and language and comprehension, amongst other needs. The team says Michael will get all the help he needs and it will be put in place as soon as possible. Although Michael is under the same bracket as Thomas, his needs are very different.

◇◇◇

William, for now, is more straightforward than his brothers. There are definitely characteristics of autism present. The difference here is that although he seems to be similar to Thomas in behaviour, William definitely seeks out eye contact. He is extremely visual, and he is buzzing to learn. It has been suggested to us that we tread carefully as to what we label him for now, as he has been allowed to complete another year in the language class. Although William will be in a senior infants setting, they are hoping that he will at least learn good behaviours

*Mick 4 Nanny William 3 Grandad Thomas 5
in 2000*

Thomas and Grandad 2000

Michael 7

Thomas 6

Thomas 8, Michael 6, Will 5

Noel and Sue 2005

Nanny, Mick 6, Will 4 ,Thomas 7, and me, Sue
Thomas Comunion in 2002

Mick 11, Grandad , Will 9 ,Noel Thomas 12, the priest, Mick my brother,
his son Luke, me Sue, Deirdre my brothers wife, and Nanny
Thomas Confirmation 2007

William 7

and routine. Hopefully, he will come to know that he has to sit down and raise his hand to answer questions and that he will be capable of at least the junior curriculum. The special needs services said they would address William next year, when his second year is due to finish, and see where he is at.

The special needs services recommends that Michael doesn't attend the same school at Thomas, as the school has done a great job with Thomas and they don't want the school to lose any confidence if Michael gets placed there. It is obvious that our lads should not be in the same school together, there would be too much competitiveness between them to the extreme of an unhealthy level. All our lads are like that at home, and I believe it is a good idea that they have time out from each other during school.

At home, Thomas is taking on the role of father figure, and with his competitiveness, he forgets to draw the line. This explains why Thomas likes to challenge me, too. We all have noticed that Thomas likes to look after his brothers; he is such a worrier. So with the problems that Thomas is having himself, if his brothers were placed in the same school and they had their own individual problems, there would be upheaval all around. For now it is not a good idea, and every year this issue will be addressed again—the problems our children are having are for the rest of their lives.

Chapter 11

Over the past couple of weeks, I have been devastated and exhausted emotionally. I have been pushed to the very edge of cracking up. Then, after thinking about the situation and facing reality, I slowly began to come around. Noel and I watched Primetime on both Monday and Tuesday, and to be honest, watching this completely knocked the stuffing out of us and we were both in shock for days. We couldn't talk to each other except for the fact that we regretted watching the programme. We were hoping that we would be enlightened as to how our boys think and feel; instead, we found out that there is absolutely no placement out there for eighteen year olds into adulthood. The placements some autistic people got were inappropriate and their medication was either insufficient or incorrect.

There are a lot of families out there who are not getting any help from services at all. It did occur to us that our family is getting help—maybe we felt that for years we were unjustified with support, but compared to other families, we did pretty well. Although we are still terrified as to what will happen when our children get older, we never want to put our children into a special home. But after what we saw on this programme, we may not have a choice. There was a family on this programme who had a teenager who hasn't received any help and can be violent when he throws a tantrum. He is a big lad too, and sometimes his father said he has to be tackled like an adult. We saw our Michael in this lad. Michael too is a big lad and throws his tantrums. I just hope and pray that when we are all older I have the strength to cope with our children. It scares me to think about the future.

◇◇◇

We got a phone call from Services, and Michael has a placement within the special school. We are delighted; however, we are going over to the school to meet everyone, and if we are happy with it, then we will apply for the placement. This is all red tape that has to be dealt with.

◇◇◇

We are delighted with the school, and it seems that all systems are go. We met some other children within the unit, and they are all lovely and have great manners—it was truly inspiring. We knew instantly that Michael would be at ease here, and there is also a buddy system, which means that Michael would never be left to his own devices. There is an older boy from the mainstream setting who will be allocated to Michael. Michael won't be walking around on his own anymore; he will have a pal.

◇◇◇

Liz (not her real name), special needs services, has been in touch with us, and there are some other people she would like to introduce to us into a local respite services house. We sat down and chatted about our children and felt very comfortable. It was suggested that these people next meet our children, and over a period of time our lads could get to know them and vice versa. We brought our lads up to the house regularly. In order not to confuse our lads, we said that this was Liam's house and some night they could stay, like a holiday from the parents.

At first I was concerned that I would be leaving my boys with strangers. I had met these people a couple of times, but did I really know them? Would our lads be okay with staying in the house? But that is why there are gazillions of questionnaires to fill out. I decided that maybe I should give these guys a chance. Our lads were always around us after all. We were being offered respite, so although I was so concerned, I knew that to be fair I had to give it a chance all round. There were other issues too, such as: would our lads settle down? Would they worry about where Mam and Dad were? What would they do if there were any emergencies? As parents, we have always been around and reliable.

◇◇◇

William just received another yellow card from school, which is definitely not good. Another lad had won a race, and William was not impressed, so he went to strangle him. Now, I know this is way out of order, but this is why I don't really like William to participate in any games. Like his brothers, he likes to win, he likes to be first—it is an obsession. We have told his teachers umpteen times about this.

This is now William's third yellow card, and he knows this is not good. William is not too familiar with the proceedings, but he definitely knows what a yellow card is and the principal was mentioned in the same sentence. William automatically got sick. His teacher told me she didn't know if he was already poorly and then this happened—she said she felt awful as to how she handled it.

We got a phone call to say William was poorly and could we collect him. Now God forbid if there was a situation in school that we needed to be aware of. William is still incapable of letting us know what has happened, due to the fact that he hasn't developed great communication skills yet. William gets so frustrated and so do we. We rely on what the teachers tell us has happened and we believe that this isn't always the full picture.

William was off for days, and he refused to eat and drink. He was getting sick and he slept a lot. We brought William to see a doctor, who couldn't find anything wrong with him but gave prescribed suppositories for both his temperature and getting sick. Over the next couple of days, there was no improvement and we were getting really worried. We made another appointment with a different doctor, who again couldn't find anything wrong.

William's primary doctor, who knows him well, was away. There was still no improvement, so I was contemplating bringing him to the hospital, but instead William had an appointment with his regular doctor, who diagnosed him with having a head cold. Due to William's autism, she said the sensation could be worse for him and gave him a mild antibiotic. He started to come around, but the next thing we knew he was lying on the sofa getting sick again.

My father suggested that William was trying to tell us something. William's lack of oral communication made it difficult to explain to us what was bothering him, so this was his way to tell us he was not happy about something. Over a period of time, rather than using my energy up on the school and trying to achieve results there while trying to be careful due to placements, I gave William all my energy to help him recover. The school term was just about up anyway. I didn't want William to be afraid to go back to school, so I sent him back for the last couple of days. William was reluctant, but I told him I would read him a story when he got home.

I sent William back with a four-page letter (not a complaint), just to say that William cannot be treated like a regular six-year-old and punished the same way. So far we have been really pussyfooting around the word autism, but the teacher was well in tune with William's diagnosis so we didn't hide it from her. Unfortunately, in order for William to get his speech and language therapy (which he badly needed), we felt that we had to be quiet about certain things. After all, the principal did say that if William had autism, then he was in the wrong placement. As parents we had developed the attitude that the school couldn't just put William out of their placement. William is legally entitled to be educated wherever that may be.

I didn't get much of a reply back, only to say that William was feeling much better. I had gone beyond the stage of caring, though. It was only when I met up with the special needs services and explained about this situation that they said that William had had an anxiety attack, which is very common with a child who has autism. They, too, agreed that it was the yellow card and the mention of the principal that triggered this attack.

Now, please don't get me wrong. I am very grateful for the therapy William is getting and will get for another year. William has come on so well since starting last year. I just feel that he is being treated unfairly and that his needs, other than the speech therapy, are not being met. William does not like crowds; he can't handle it. He is very competitive and is still unable to communicate to the level of any other six and half year old. But we as parents have to ignore the fact that William has autism to a degree for now and that includes misbehaviour and concentration issues. It is very frustrating for us, but we know by William's behaviour that he gets frustrated, too.

Chapter 12

◇ ◇ ◇◇ ◇ ◇◇ ◇ ◇◇ ◇ ◇◇

Now let me fill you in to date. "There's more?" I hear you say. Well, just to enlighten you, this situation is never-ending and never will be. We have been to meet the crew that will work with us through Respite, and we have filled out the forms they requested. When we were told we could have two nights respite, we were so excited and delighted that we were beside ourselves. We brought up our lads' favourite toys, extra clothes, and whatever food they needed. We dropped our children off, and I wasn't sure how I felt. We came home to a very quiet house: there was no screaming, crying, or loud noise. It really felt weird.

We were told that we could do whatever we liked, and of course, if there were any problems we could ring anytime. Due to the fact that this was the first time too for our lads to be away from home and away from their parents, we decided that to ease the situation we would bring our lads to their usual appointments. We could have a free night, but we had to get up early to collect our boys.

On our first night alone, Noel and I sat at the kitchen table with the biggest grins on our faces. We literally didn't know what to do with our free time; we hadn't had quality time since Thomas was born. But never mind, we soon got ideas, which we were both still grinning about from ear to ear (I'm sure you know what I mean). Later on, we decided to order food and watch a DVD with the sound up (usually we keep it quiet as we are trying to get our boys to sleep).

I was expecting the phone to ring at any time, but it didn't. It felt so weird not having our boys at home that at one point I shouted up the stairs for them to go to sleep, which made me feel a little better, we got an early night and we didn't realise how exhausted we were until we got the respite. Our lads have only ever had us and we have devoted our lives to them.

The next day, after our usual running around, we dropped our lads off for their second night and again we were exhausted but we decided to make the most of our last night. So we went out to dinner and watched a DVD when we came home. We were home by 10 p.m., but we really enjoyed it. We were told by Respite that our lads were fine; they were awake up until about midnight, which is pretty normal for them.

We were told that we could have respite again, and we were delighted. We did get a phone call recently saying that there was room available for two of our three boys and would we be interested? We declined, saying it wouldn't be fair for whichever one of our children would be left out. How could this be explained to him? Respite agreed with us, but because we didn't get respite this month, Liz has kindly organised it so that our lads are looked after for a couple of hours. We are delighted to make the most of these opportunities.

Liz has been so supportive since we met her. She rings regularly to see if there is anything she can do to help. Liz organised it for Thomas to go to summer camp for a couple of days while Michael was at his summer camp. She also had a person call our home to set up resource teaching for Thomas and another girl to help him with social skills and interaction. And then we have gotten to meet other families with children with autism. Liz was coordinator of all this, and she has done a great job.

I have probably mentioned this already, but again it is a great relief to sit down and talk to someone who understands our fears and frustrations. We are grateful to all these people who have helped us out lately; it brings a sense of happiness to our hearts. We are told that we have three nights respite within the next couple of weeks, and we can't wait. Those in charge who we initially met, said that we can go off somewhere for the first night but the second night might be a different situation, as we are all aware that our lads might get a bit boisterous. We wholeheartedly agreed.

The furthest we are comfortable traveling is up to my family in Tallaght. A party has been organised in Carlow where the rest of my family is. We are still nervous leaving our lads overnight and going such a long distance. In case of emergency, it would be easier to get a taxi from Tallaght to Meath, rather than Carlow to Meath. At the same time, I am really looking forward to it.

◇◇◇

I have been reading this book called LD Child and the ADHD Child http://www.amazon.com/LD-Child-ADHD-Parents-Professionals/dp/0895871424, which is one I would recommend. It is very educational about the problems our boys have and gives great suggestions on how to help them. One thing baffles me, though. We received forms from the services to be completed and there was a question on it regarding LD. I wasn't sure what exactly the question meant, so I decided to ring Services and ask them if it had any connection with ASD.

There are similarities all right, but I didn't see the facts. Well, it was explained to me that our children do indeed have learning disabilities and they come under the heading Autism Spectrum Disorder. Our lads will always have their problems, but now all of a sudden I understand. How could I have been so blind? It's simple—it could happen to anyone. For years we have been fighting for our children, for their needs to be recognised, and we have been asking the same questions over and over again and again.

The main thing is that now I know. I don't fully understand why our boys do what they do. What is so nice about this visual stimulation? Why must things be done the same way day in and day out? But I am aware of the areas our children have their difficulties in, and now I can help. I am sure there are people we have helped along our lives. We don't fully understand the complexities of autism, but we help anyway.

Conclusion

will keep you informed of their progress as our children are getting older. It is not all doom and gloom; there is light at the end of the tunnel, and life is not so bad. For the first time in a long time, I can actually say that I am happy, Noel is happy, and our boys are happy. As I said before, the situation at home has never changed; it is us as parents who have changed. Is it closure? Honestly, I don't know. We have answers now, and we are getting help with and for the boys. I think finally we know that our boys have always had difficulties and problems. It wasn't our imagination; we are not cracking up. There are a lot of plans in the works to help our lads and they are to be put in place soon.

It has been a long, exhausting battle, but we are there now. Our lads will need help for the rest of their lives. We will see how it goes—you can only take it day by day. We have all progressed, physically and mentally, and now I know there is hope for our boys. Who knows—their dreams may yet come true. Thomas wants to be a professional footballer, Michael wants to be palaeontologist, and William wants to become a police officer.

My children have asked me lately what it was like as a family growing up with this autism. I gave them this diary that I have been writing personal notes in over the years and told them to read it. All three of my lads said that I should publish it, as it may help other families, and they said it was very good. I found a written attachment at the end of the pages written by my son William, now age sixteen. It says:

"This book is inspiring, emotional, and irreplaceable, it's about us three kids: the youngest is me at age seven at the last record. We have put Noel and Sue through a lot, they had a lot to deal with, and I can say that all the support, help, and understanding has finally paid off. Why? Because in 2013, after being reassessed, I was told I now have PDD-NOS (pervasive development disorder not otherwise specified), which I'm told means that basically my autism is so mild, you wouldn't really know it is there. It is so mild that you could say I no longer have autism. I was told by the lady who assessed me my autism is gone, I am so happy now. I love you lots, Sue and Noel. Thank you for all you have done for us."

William xxx

The future for my lads is bright now, and there is hope. My fear of the unknown is not so bad. And as for my lads, well, my dreams are that their dreams come true. Although there are still issues with communication and understanding all 3 lads have the potential (with a little guidance) of achieving their goals. The sky is the limit; the lads can now be seen as the beautiful individual young men they have become, hence the title: "from a moth to a butterfly."

◇◇◇

Thomas 12, Jemma, Aunty Marie, Mick 11,
William 9, and Noel in 2007

Thomas 15, Will 12, Mick 13

A wonderful day with my remarkable family, here are my brothers, sisters, their partners, inlaws and outlaws haha, from left to right: Jemma, my niece; Siobhan, my nephew's partner; Ali, my baby sister; Martin, her partner; Pat, my brother-in-law; Deo, my Mammy, and Mick, my Dad; my nephew; Roy Junior, my nephew; Paul, my baby brother; Joe right in the middle is the Wedding couple; Hanna with Micka, my younger brother; Luke, their son; Roy Senior, my brother-in-law; Debbie, my sister; myself; William, my son, 12, Uncle Pat with his wife Aunty Gerry, Noel, my darling husband; Thomas 14; and Mick 13.

Thomas 18

Michael 16

Will 16, Mick 18, Thomas 19

William 17

If you loved this book, would you please
submit a review at Amazon.com?

Lightning Source UK Ltd.
Milton Keynes UK
UKOW03f0723110517

300979UK00001B/20/P